ROBERT RAUSCHENBERG

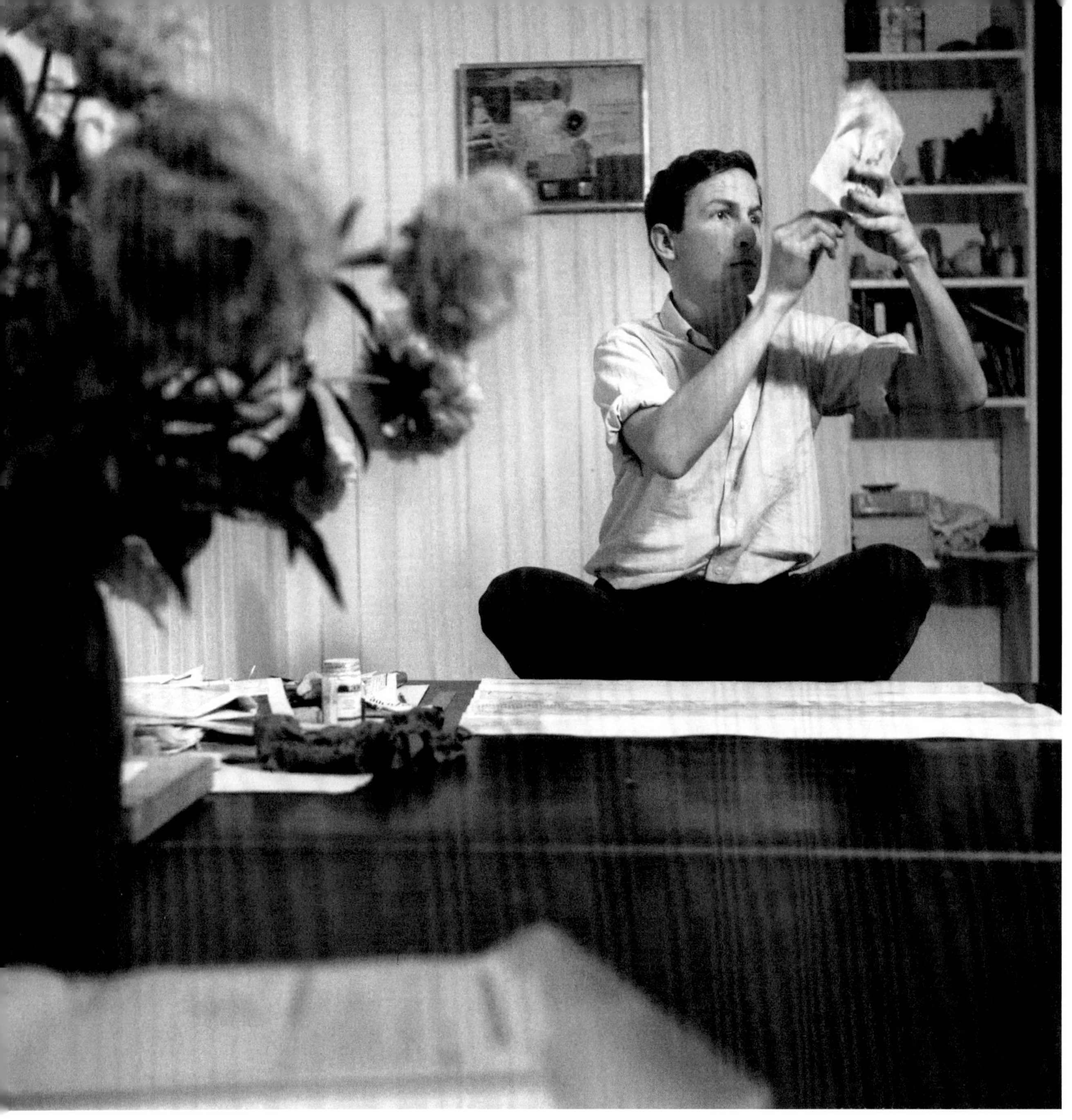

ROBERT RAUSCHENBERG

Thirty-Four Illustrations for Dante's *Inferno*

Essay by
Leah Dickerman

Poetry by
Robin Coste Lewis
Kevin Young

THE MUSEUM OF MODERN ART
New York

MMXVII

This publication is made possible through a grant from the Robert Rauschenberg Foundation.

Major support is provided by the Riva Castleman Fund for Publications in the Department of Drawings and Prints, established by The Derald H. Ruttenberg Foundation.

Published by The Museum of Modern Art
11 West 53 Street, New York, New York 10019
www.moma.org

Produced by the Department of Publications,
The Museum of Modern Art, New York
Christopher Hudson, Publisher
Chul R. Kim, Associate Publisher
David Frankel, Editorial Director
Marc Sapir, Production Director

Edited by Maria Marchenkova
Designed by Amanda Washburn
Production by Marc Sapir
Printed and bound by Ofset Yapimevi, Istanbul
This book is typeset in Vendetta.
The paper is 150 gsm Garda Matt Ultra.

Distributed in the United States and Canada by
ARTBOOK | D.A.P.
155 Sixth Avenue, 2nd Floor, New York, New York 10013
www.artbook.com

Distributed outside the United States and Canada by
Thames & Hudson Ltd.
181a High Holborn, London WC1V 7QX
www.thamesandhudson.com

Library of Congress Control Number: 2017936943
ISBN: 978-1-63345-029-5

Printed in Turkey

Photograph Credits

Courtesy Archives of American Art, Smithsonian Institution: figs. 1, 2. Courtesy The Brant Foundation, Greenwich, Connecticut: fig. 4. Courtesy Moderna Museet, Stockholm: fig. 3. The Museum of Modern Art, Department of Imaging Services, photo Thomas Griesel: p. 6, pp. 26–92; photo John Wronn: fig. 8. Courtesy Robert Rauschenberg Foundation Archives, New York: back cover; p. 2; p. 8; figs. 6, 7. Courtesy True Temper Sports: fig. 8. © 2017 The Andy Warhol Foundation for the Visual Arts, Inc./Artists Rights Society (ARS), New York: fig. 4.

Front cover: Robert Rauschenberg. *Canto XIV: Circle Seven, Round 3, the Violent against God, Nature, and Art* from the series Thirty-Four Illustrations for Dante's *Inferno*. See p. 53

Back cover: Robert Rauschenberg, 1958. Detail of a photograph by Jasper Johns. Robert Rauschenberg Foundation Archives, New York

P. 2: Rauschenberg working on a solvent transfer drawing in his Front Street studio, New York, 1958. Work in background is Untitled (1955). Photograph: Jasper Johns. Photograph Collection. Robert Rauschenberg Foundation Archives, New York.

P. 6: Robert Rauschenberg. *Canto XXXI: The Central Pit of Malebolge, the Giants* (detail) from the series Thirty-Four Illustrations for Dante's *Inferno*. See p. 87

CONTENTS

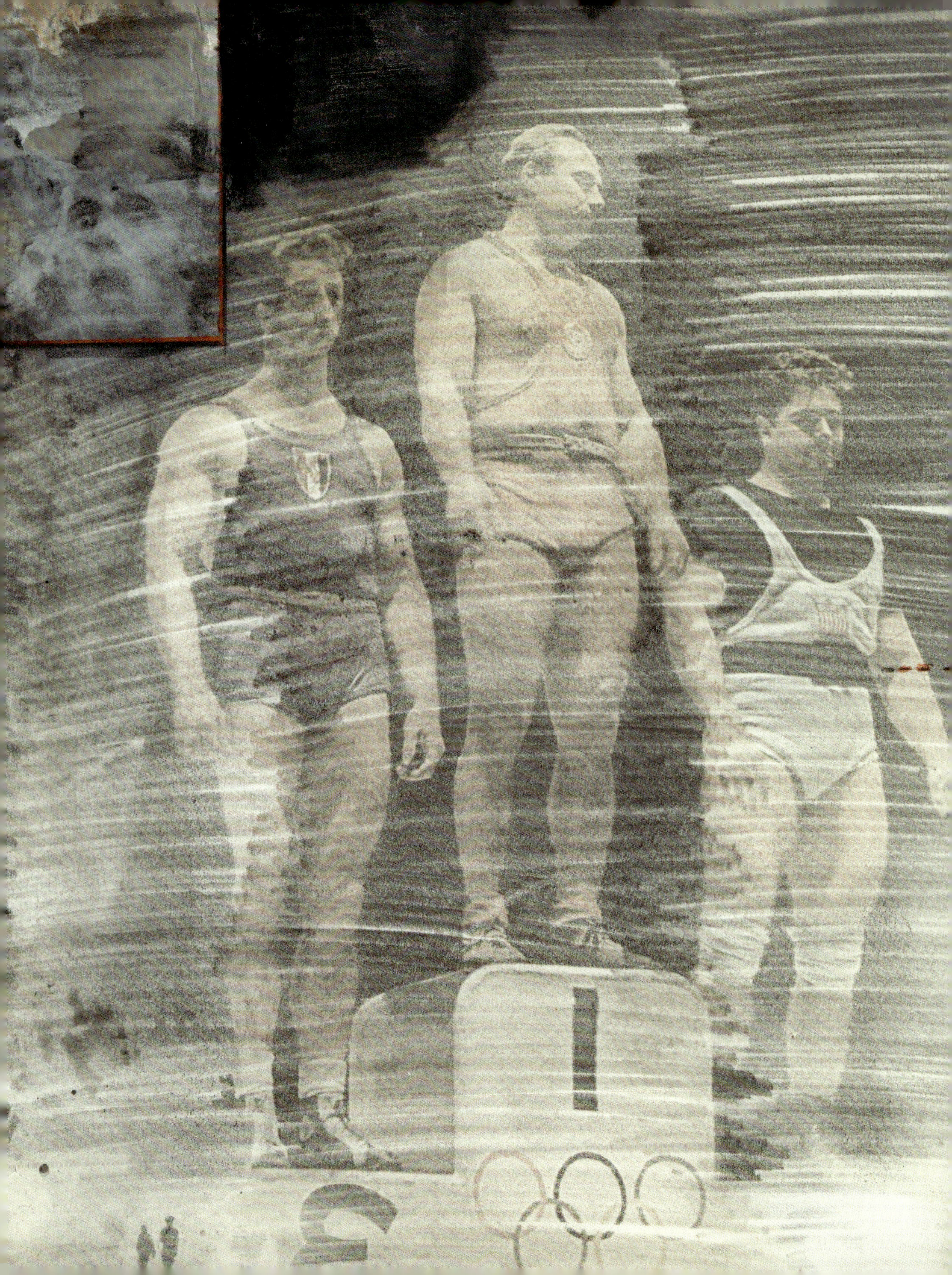

Foreword

Dante Alighieri was in his mid-thirties when he began writing the *Inferno*, as Robert Rauschenberg was when he began working on his series of drawings illustrating each canto of Dante's epic journey through the netherworld. Rauschenberg worked on it in strict chronological order, canto by canto as he read, and the project occupied him—even when he paused his work on it—for over two and a half years. The result is Rauschenberg's most sustained exercise in the medium of drawing. It was surprising to observers when the series was first displayed in 1960, after avant-garde painters in New York had embraced abstraction for almost two decades, that Rauschenberg, a rising star, had chosen to journey into the symbolic universe of Dante's Hell. Acquired by The Museum of Modern Art soon after its making through an anonymous gift, Rauschenberg's Thirty-Four Illustrations for Dante's *Inferno* is now among the most celebrated works in our drawings collection. It is with pride that we publish this volume on the occasion of our retrospective of the artist's career, *Robert Rauschenberg: Among Friends*.

Rauschenberg was always a great experimenter. For the Dante series, rather than making conventional drawings, he used a novel technique that allowed him to capture images from the media-saturated reality of the contemporary world. He moistened clippings from photo-illustrated magazines with solvent and rubbed their backs with an implement to transfer them to drawing paper. He then added washes of watercolor and gouache, touches of crayon, chalk, and pencil, combining traditional fine art materials with these migrant glyphs from the media world. He described the results as "combine drawings." They can also be seen as an early salvo in a revolution: the use of readymade images would serve as the foundation for Pop art in the decade to come.

The ghostly images aptly evoke the shades of Dante's world. Yet they are also sharply contemporary, referencing current events, creating an allusive relay between the classical world and Rauschenberg's present. Like Dante's *Inferno* before them, they weave together meditations on both public and private spheres, politics and inner life. It is perhaps the searching of an artist who, approaching the end of youth, is pushing himself to greater wisdom and comprehension of the world around him. And it is a poignant and haunting vision of hell, of souls condemned to eternal suffering by sins both great and small, of human imperfection and vulnerability.

Above all, Rauschenberg's Dante drawings pay homage to creativity in dialogue. The ancient Roman poet Virgil's *Aeneid* was both source and model for Dante's tale. Virgil accompanies Dante, as mentor and guide, on his journey into hell. Rauschenberg chose Dante for his own odyssey; each drawing is a conversation with the poet across the centuries.

Now, we have asked two extraordinary poets of our own time—Kevin Young and Robin Coste Lewis—to offer their response, in conversation with each other, to Rauschenberg's Thirty-Four Illustrations for Dante's *Inferno*. We are delighted to be able to share their work: a poem for each drawing.

We would like to extend our sincere thanks to the writers, including Leah Dickerman, The Marlene Hess Curator of Painting and Sculpture, MoMA; to our Department of Drawings and Prints and our Department of Publications; and to the Sonnabend family. We are deeply grateful to the Robert Rauschenberg Foundation for making this project possible and to The Derald H. Ruttenberg Foundation for establishing the Riva Castleman Fund for Publications, which is supporting this publication.

GLENN D. LOWRY
Director, The Museum of Modern Art

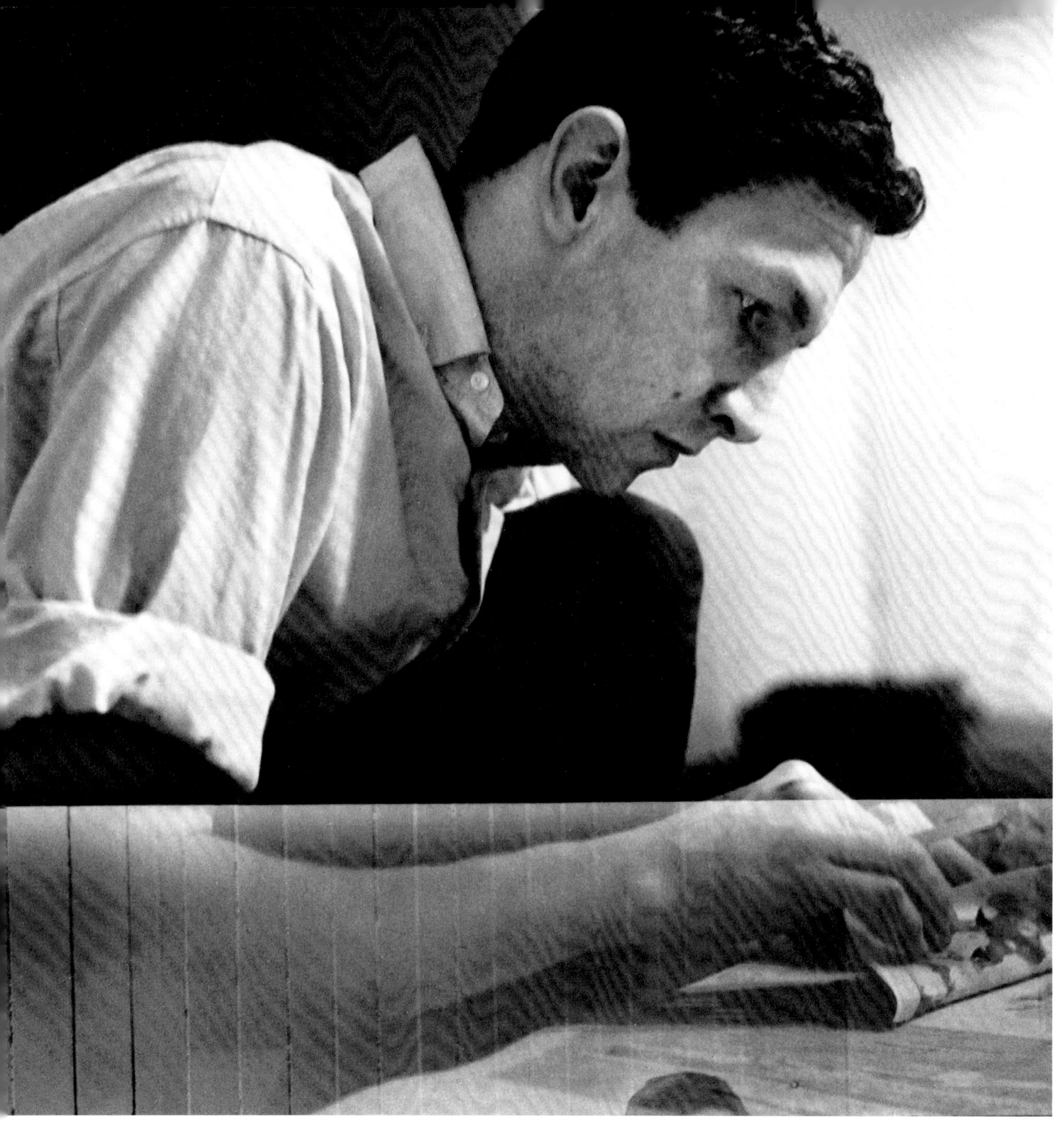

Rauschenberg working on a solvent transfer drawing
in his Front Street studio, New York, 1958.
Photograph: Jasper Johns. Photograph Collection. Robert Rauschenberg
Foundation Archives, New York

Canto by Canto
An Introduction

Leah Dickerman

It began when Robert Rauschenberg decided to "make a whole lot of drawings," he recounted, so he started "looking for a vehicle, something to keep them going."[1] Propelled by his desire to focus on the medium in depth, Rauschenberg set to work in the middle of 1958 on a series of drawings inspired by Dante Alighieri's *Inferno*, the first of the poet's three-part epic *Divina Commedia* (*Divine Comedy*, c. 1307–21). He proceeded to make one drawing for each of the *Inferno*'s thirty-four cantos, culling images from popular illustrated magazines using a novel solvent transfer technique, then adding touches of pencil, crayon, watercolor wash, and gouache. He continued working on the project, with breaks and varying intensity, across two and a half years, through the end of 1960, when the series was presented at the Leo Castelli Gallery in New York (fig. 1).

Working from a literary source was a first for the artist, one that he spoke of as a "test."[2] "The problem when I started the Dante illustrations was to see if I was working abstractly because I couldn't work any other way or whether I was doing it by choice," the artist explained to Dorothy Gees Seckler. "So I insisted on the challenge of being restricted by a particular subject where it meant that I'd have to be involved in symbolism. . . . Well, I spent two-and-a-half years deciding that, yes, I could do that."[3] It may seem surprising that for this test against narrative constraint the young artist chose a work written more than six centuries before, one telling of the poet-narrator's visionary journey through the spiritual realms of Hell and Purgatory, where he is accompanied by the ancient Roman poet Virgil, and Heaven, where he continues alone.

The sheer tenacity of Rauschenberg's pursuit over a long period of time stands out, as do the suggestions of emotional strain that appear in his descriptions of efforts to bring the series to completion, so

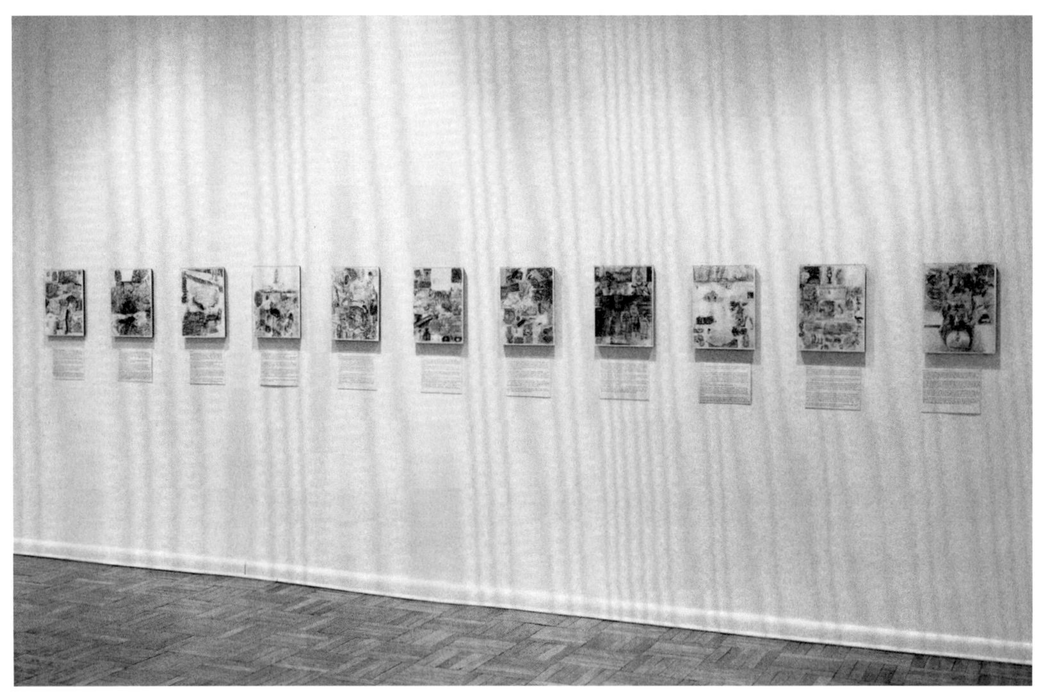

1.34 *Illustrations for Dante's Inferno* exhibition, Leo Castelli Gallery, New York, December 6, 1960–January 7, 1961. Installation view showing Rauschenberg's drawings for Cantos XXIV–XXXIV, with Michael Sonnabend's narrative summaries below. Archives of American Art, Smithsonian Institution

atypical for this artist who generally spoke lightly, even playfully, of the process of making art. Rauschenberg had consistently rejected the trope of psychic struggle in creation that was so pervasive among an older generation of Abstract Expressionist painters. "There was a whole language that I could never make function for myself in relationship to painting," he explained. "Attitudes like tortured, struggle, pain. . . . I never could see those qualities in paint."[4] Nonetheless, after receiving a rejection from the John Simon Guggenheim Memorial Foundation for a fellowship to support work on the project, he seems to have encountered doubt. He had applied after completing the first six drawings, throwing himself into preparing the application during the fall of 1958, carefully crafting his statement and soliciting references from luminaries in his world like MoMA curator Dorothy Miller, publisher George Wittenborn, and Dante's new translator, the poet John Ciardi, while refraining from asking artists who might be too forward-thinking for the respectable Guggenheim committee.[5] Rauschenberg would recount to the critic Calvin Tomkins that he had approached Ciardi with the first group of drawings in hand, and the poet agreed to recommend him, though seemingly reluctantly, saying that "he didn't know why, he'd always thought of the *Inferno* as all dark."[6] When Rauschenberg got the disappointing news from the foundation, he put the project aside. He picked it up again some time later, forging ahead without grant support, simultaneously working on several exhibitions, dance collaborations, and a contribution to Jean Tinguely's *Homage to New York*, a machine staged to self-destruct in the Sculpture Garden of The Museum of Modern Art in 1960. The impact of his immersion in Dante registered in the Combines made in this period, which are rife with references to the classical world: *Gift for Apollo* (1959) conjures the Sun God's daily chariot ride in the sky; *Canyon* (1959) recasts the myth of Zeus's descent to earth in the guise of an eagle in order to capture the beautiful Ganymede; and *Winter Pool* (1959) evokes Narcissus's tale of echoes and mirrored reflections (fig. 2). Amid all this activity, Rauschenberg concluded that in order to see the *Inferno* project through he needed to withdraw from his normal routine, isolate himself from human demands—the phone calls, the broken hearts needing consolation—and all the enmeshments of a social world that he usually embraced with open arms, and leave New York City. In mid-1960, he traveled to Treasure Island, off the coast of St. Petersburg, Florida, and there worked in near solitude: "It was exactly what I needed. I stayed there six months, and I never knew anyone. I did the last half of it there. The Inferno builds up in intensity, and I really needed the isolation."[7] Returning to New York at the end of 1960, he showed the completed series at the Leo Castelli Gallery from December 6, 1960, to January 7, 1961. Critics seemed to struggle to make sense of the rising star's engagement with Dante's symbolic domain. Stuart Preston, for one, wrote in the *New York Times*, "They can be criticized for being too literary and for containing too many superficial and ephemeral conceits that do not pass successfully as images. But his attempt is a brave one, and, in its odd way, moving."[8]

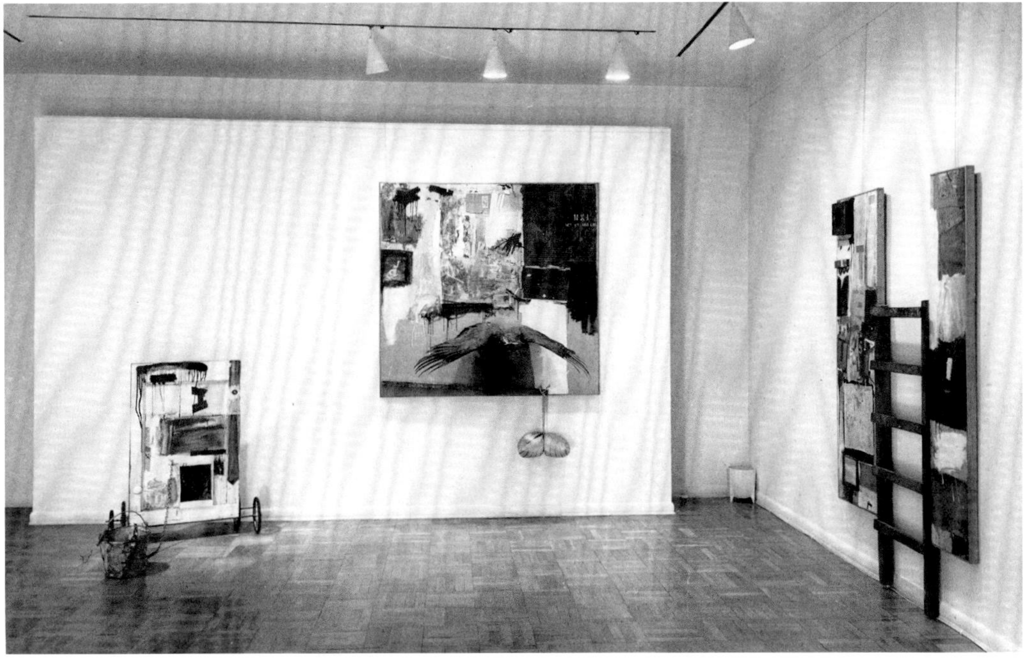

2. *Robert Rauschenberg* exhibition, Leo Castelli Gallery, New York, March 29–April 16, 1960. Installation view, left to right: *Gift for Apollo*, *Canyon*, and *Winter Pool*, all 1959. Photograph: Rudy Burckhardt. Archives of American Art, Smithsonian Institution

In making the Dante drawings, Rauschenberg soaked images taken from *Sports Illustrated*, *Time*, *Life*, and other photo-illustrated magazines with lighter fluid, which functioned as a solvent, then pressed the clippings facedown on a sheet of paper, rubbing their backs with the barrel of an empty ballpoint pen. The transferred images appeared in reverse, at the same scale as the mass-media originals, but with a fainter palette—for only some of the ink was dislodged in this second-generation printing—and in broken striations resulting from the rubbing. He then worked further on each drawing, adding strokes of pencil and crayon, washes of watercolor and gouache, and occasionally pasting on collage elements. The ghostly palette and the broken markings give the images a certain tenuous materiality, a sense of coming in and out of being, which has been described as "veiling."[9] Their shadowy presence aptly evokes the shades who inhabit Dante's netherworld. Branden Joseph has also perceptively likened this aspect of the works to the flickering of the low-resolution screens of the era's television sets, one of which always seemed to keep Rauschenberg company. The visual consonance with the new medium of television offers a frame of reference for the flow of media images that appear in his drawings.[10] Such reproduction of the media image as trace, and something worked on, also has the effect of rendering it as touched. In this way, the Dante illustrations seem allied with work being done at this time by Jasper Johns, then Rauschenberg's partner, such as *Painted Bronze* (1960), a pair of ordinary ale cans meticulously remade in modeled bronze and painted by hand.

The technique he used in making the drawings, Rauschenberg later recalled to Tomkins, was obvious to him: "I got to that right away. I already had that."[11] He had, he said, experimented with transferring printed images on a trip he made to Cuba with fellow artist Cy Twombly during a spring break from Black Mountain College in 1952. According to his description, however, in those early works the images were transferred dry, without any solvent, and culled from comic strips—clippings from the funnies like those that appeared in the proto-Combine Red Paintings he made soon afterward, including works such as *Yoicks* and *Minutiae* (both 1954)—and other graphic print sources, rather than photographic ones, as in the Dante series. This first Cuban trial with transferring images came out of his desire to find a mode of working in the medium of drawing analogous to the one he had defined for himself in painting, which brought the stuff of the world into his works. "I liked the intimacy of drawing against the object quality of my painting," he would explain. "I'd always liked to draw.... But I felt I had to find a way to use collage in drawing, to incorporate my own way of working on that intimate scale. I said I wouldn't come back from Cuba until I had found it, and luckily I did."[12] After having discovered it, however, Rauschenberg set the technique aside for more than five years, only returning to it in early 1958, when, immediately before launching into the Dante series, he began making a suite of transfer drawings, now using a solvent, experimenting first with turpentine, then settling on lighter fluid, and choosing photo-based imagery for application. The process, through dissolution and friction, made images mobile, capable of flight from one support to another, one discursive sphere to another.

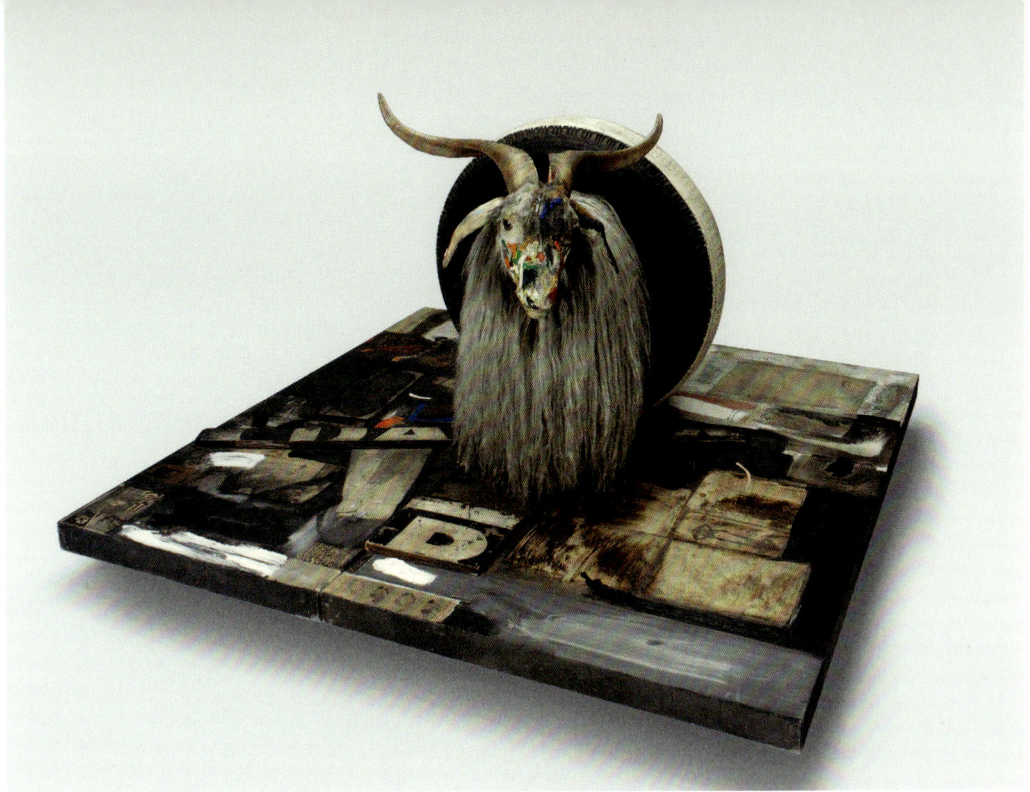

3. Robert Rauschenberg. *Monogram*. 1955–59. Oil, paper, fabric, printed reproductions, metal, wood, rubber shoe-heel, and tennis ball on two conjoined canvases with oil on taxidermied Angora goat with brass plaque and rubber tire on wood platform mounted on four casters, 42 x 53 1/4 x 64 1/2 in. (106.7 x 135.2 x 163.8 cm). Moderna Museet, Stockholm. Purchase with contribution from Moderna Museets Vänner/The Friends of Moderna Museet

Photo-based media had already entered Rauschenberg's work in clippings glued to the surfaces of Combines such as *Canyon* (1959) and *Monogram* (1955–59) (fig. 3); with his transfer drawings, photomechanical images plucked from the flux of contemporary culture became central. The Dante project provided Rauschenberg with what the art historian Rosalind Krauss has described as "his apprenticeship to the media image,"[13] training in the strategic premises of what would become known as Pop art.[14] The Dante drawings led Rauschenberg almost immediately to efforts to scale up, to create a painting with readymade images: the artist first made *Calendar*, a solvent "transfer painting," in 1962, which he felt was not fully successful in the way that the magazine images were dwarfed by the large canvas; he then attempted and failed to find a way to produce photo-sensitive canvas that would allow images to be imprinted directly onto the support;[15] and finally—after consulting with Andy Warhol, who had just begun making silkscreen paintings—he adopted the silkscreen technique himself (figs. 4, 5). "Silkscreen was a way not to be victimized and limited in scale and color, but still have access to current worldwide information," he would explain in 1997 in comments he made on an essay about his work that Krauss was preparing for publication.[16] Combining photography and painting, machine work and manual work, these early silkscreens registered images of culture at large but also reflected on the tradition of fine-art painting. In Rauschenberg's case, the move from collaged abstraction to media-based imagery came via Dante.

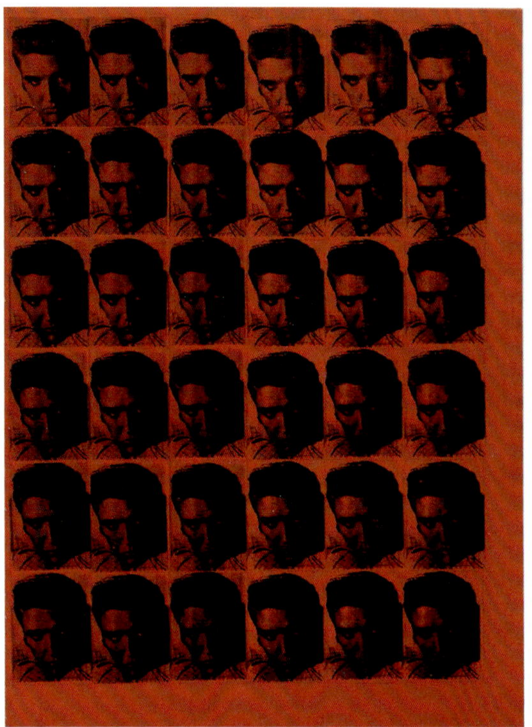

4. Andy Warhol. *Red Elvis*. 1962.
Silkscreen ink and acrylic on linen,
69 3/4 x 52 in. (177.2 x 132.1 cm).
The Brant Foundation, Greenwich, Connecticut

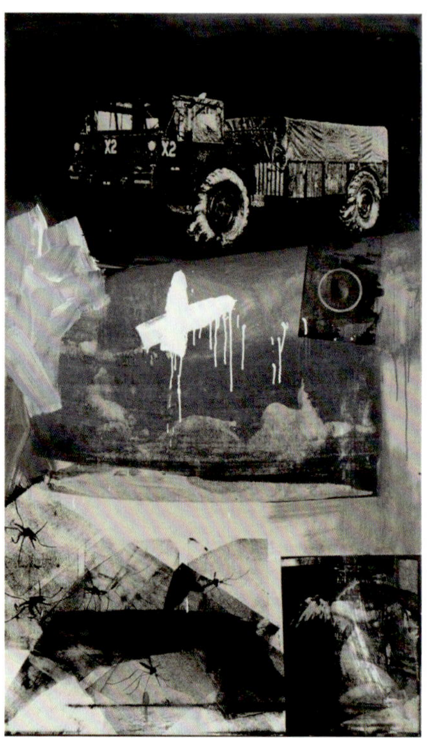

5. Robert Rauschenberg. *Crocus*. 1962.
Oil and silkscreen-ink print on canvas,
60 x 36 in. (152.4 x 91.4 cm). Private collection

When Rauschenberg began work on the series, he had never read the *Inferno*.[17] He later recalled that when Alfred H. Barr, Jr., chief curator at The Museum of Modern Art, and Dorothy Miller, the curator charged with contemporary art, arrived to visit his dealer Leo Castelli, they brought a copy of Dante's *Inferno*.[18] The occasion may well have been a viewing of Rauschenberg's first exhibition at Castelli's gallery, in early 1958, where he debuted his Combines, paintings which incorporated all manner of materials—a taxidermied chicken, a pair of shoes, a baseball, a pillow, a door—sometimes things so large and unwieldy that the work became, as Rauschenberg put it, "awkward physically."[19] Barr and Miller originally declined to buy any of the Combines, a decision that lingered as a slight in Rauschenberg's mind.[20] Indeed, of the twenty works shown, only *Bed* (1955) was bought, and by Castelli himself. The remembrance says something about the cultured world in which Rauschenberg—who hailed from the gulf town of Port Arthur, Texas, and had little formal literary education—had found himself. Castelli was a Trieste-born refugee from Europe's recent convulsions. Ileana Sonnabend—his wife, a key figure at the Castelli Gallery, and later, with the founding of her own gallery in Paris in 1962, Rauschenberg's European dealer—was the daughter of one of Romania's prewar textile magnates. Both were multilingual, witty, urbane, and wide-ranging in their cultural interests. By the time Rauschenberg began his Dante project in 1958, Leo and Ileana were moving toward separation, though their lives would remain closely entwined. Ileana had found a new companion in Michael Sonnabend, an "emigre from Buffalo," as he described himself,[21] with an elfin mien, a bright laugh, and an unmistakable voice; they married in 1959. Sonnabend was a self-taught scholar of the Italian Renaissance: he had traveled to Venice as a young man to learn to read Dante in the original. Nina Sundell, Leo and Ileana's daughter, would remember how the relics of classic European culture pervaded the conversational rituals of this modern family: "Michael [Sonnabend] and Leo would recite Dante; Marianne [Nina's oldest daughter] knew La Fontaine and the letters of Madame de Sévigné."[22] One senses the potency of Dante's immaterial presence for Rauschenberg in 1958, when he was tightly enmeshed with Castelli and the Sonnabends and harboring hopes of an acquisition by MoMA.

At the same time, Dante was receiving fresh attention from American audiences, sparked by the publication in 1954 of Ciardi's new translation, which offered English terza rima verses to those who did not have access to the Italian original. Published in both deluxe hardcover and paperback editions, it was enthusiastically embraced, selling nearly sixty thousand copies in its first six months.[23] The muscular contemporaneity of Ciardi's verse earned critics' acclaim. In the *New York Times*, underscoring what he perceived as the masculinity of both Ciardi's prose and the figure of the translator himself, Dudley Fitts proclaimed with considerable fanfare:

My few sessions with John Ciardi have been anything but those of sweet silent thought: I have quarreled with him about his rhyme, his meter and his diction, and my neighbors still meditate upon our discussion of the first line of the last Canto, which consumed the better part of an evening and involved considerable breakage of furniture.... Nevertheless, I feel now what I have felt from the beginning: that here is our Dante, Dante for the first time translated into virile, tense American verse.[24]

A comparison with British author Dorothy Sayers's translation—a mass-market competitor to Ciardi's, first published in 1949—of Francesca's famous lines about Paolo in Canto V makes the frank, carnal urgency of Ciardi's rendering appreciable.

Sayers: *Love, that to no loved heart remits love's score,*
Took me with such great joy of him, that see!
It holds me yet and never shall leave me more.[25]

Ciardi: *Love, which permits no loved one not to love,*
Took me so strongly with delight in him
That we are one in Hell, as we were above.[26]

Although Rauschenberg bought several translations—everything he could find on the shelves of a secondhand bookstore on Fourth Avenue, he later reported in an interview with Barbara Rose[27]—it was Ciardi's that resonated with him.

Ciardi's translation is accompanied by extensive footnote annotations, also appealingly lucid and down-to-earth, for example, identifying the historical figures on whom Dante based his characters Paolo and Francesca as an adulterous thirteenth-century couple from Ravenna, with the introduction "The facts are these."[28] Ciardi's notes placed him (as Rauschenberg's drawings would later place him) in a nearly seven-hundred-year-long tradition of commentary on the *Inferno* that began almost as soon as Dante had finished writing it and which goes on to this day. Such commentary was necessary, poet Clive James explains in his introduction to a recent verse translation of the *Inferno*, because "Dante had composed every canto of his poem as if it were a weekend article based on news that only just happened, and whose details did not need to be outlined."[29] Rauschenberg was also aware that many artists had illustrated Dante's narrative journey through hell in a form of visual commentary on the poet's work—that Michelangelo had made drawings, which were later lost at sea; that Gustave Doré had created an etching series, which was not to Rauschenberg's taste; and that Botticelli, too, had tackled the subject, producing drawings that Rauschenberg called "his favorite" for the way the artist had treated the material "like a combination road map and cartoon."[30] It was a noble lineage, and the dialogue between artist and writer appealed to him: "An illustration has to be read: it has to relate to something already in existence."[31]

In tackling the task he had set for himself, Rauschenberg put in place a number of rules for engagement with the poetic text. He would make one drawing for each of the thirty-four cantos, illustrating all rather than selecting scenes the way previous illustrators of the series had done, which he thought put too much emphasis on the artist's discernment.[32] He would make each drawing immediately after reading the relevant canto, and without reading ahead. This one-at-a-time rule seemed aimed at ensuring that Rauschenberg encountered the changing story line afresh, responding in the present, despite the span of hundreds of years. He structured time as a factor in another way, too, by largely limiting himself to culling images from magazines on the stands at that moment, so that Dante's narrative sequence was given counterpoint in the shifting register of current events—the present of each canto was matched with a contemporary moment in time. All of the drawings were made on paper of the same stock, 14 ½ x 11 ½ inch Strathmore, which was a bit larger than a book page but similarly intimate in the way it was to be read. The scale of the components of the drawings were to be tied to the author's words, treated in proportion to the role they play in the text: "The space allowed for each image was a measure made by the space occupied by the author's words, literally," he later explained to Krauss. "I was the reporter."[33] In Canto XXXI, for example, the poets encounter the Giants, who appear to Dante as towers in the dark before he realizes that they are actually men of extraordinary size, whose grotesque features are then inventoried and measured in the text at length. Accordingly, in Rauschenberg's drawing for the canto, Olympic wrestlers on the medal stand fill more than half the page, more space than any other transferred image. Each of these constraints—of comprehensiveness, time, scale, proportionality—allowed Dante's text to structure the way that Rauschenberg worked, to make demands on his production. He held on to the relationship between text and image in the first presentation of the drawings, at Castelli's gallery in December 1960, hanging short typescript narrative summaries by Michael Sonnabend under each work. Sonnabend later recalled that Rauschenberg had approached Ciardi to ask if he might write something "so that people would know the story when they looked at the pictures," but Ciardi declared that he hated the young artist's work, and Sonnabend volunteered instead.[34]

Rauschenberg was severely dyslexic and did not read much. As he described in a conversation with Maxime de la Falaise McKendry, "When I'm writing, I know what I'm writing; when I'm reading, I can't see it because it goes from all sides of the page at once."[35] One can see the Dante drawings—whose images spin within an inchoate space—as literalizing the artist's experience of reading. Yet he did read the *Inferno*, Michael Sonnabend later emphasized, recounting, with a twinkle in his voice, that "he was going to be erudite like the rest of us."[36] Sonnabend was frequently present as the artist worked on the series. They discussed the text at length and worked on compositional schemas. And it seems that Sonnabend often read the cantos aloud to Rauschenberg.[37] Later, when Sonnabend began creating the summaries of the cantos, he saw the task as "giving the meaning where [Rauschenberg] introduced these things," writing "every day, 34 days, one a day. That's the way we did it."[38] One can imagine that Sonnabend's role as interlocutor, reader, and collaborator put the process back into a conversational mode more comfortable for Rauschenberg. The relationship provided Rauschenberg with a living avatar of Dante, allowing the artist to collaborate with the poet across time. Dore Ashton similarly recalled that when she was writing an essay introduction to the deluxe printed edition of the drawings published by Harry N. Abrams in 1964, she and Rauschenberg

read the poem together, speaking about Dante's ineffable pride, his sly witticisms, his digs at his artistic rivals, his occasional pique and silliness… his political shrewdness, his lyrical abandon, his extraordinary feeling for the particular, his forthright language, and above all his great artistic consistencies.[39]

The images of Sonnabend declaiming Dante's verses, and of Rauschenberg and Ashton reading together, are in keeping with the way Dante's contemporaries would have heard the *Inferno*. In his time, as in Virgil's before him, poems were read aloud in public more than in solitude. The production of manuscripts was expensive, and only with the development of a modern print culture did silent reading become the norm.[40] Poetry was thus an acoustic art. Dante himself was a vivid public speaker and reader, noted for his ability to entertain and his talent as a mimic.[41] He highlighted the aural quality of his text in choosing to write not in the Latin of the educated classes but in the vernacular dialect of Tuscany—language as it was spoken. He deployed a roster of effects that evoke the sounds of contemporary life, shifts in dialect and speaking style, all evincing a keen awareness of the relationship between author and listening public. And, of course, much of the *Inferno* is framed as a running conversation between Dante and Virgil, his guide and companion through the underworld, whose *Aeneid* was both source and model for Dante's own narrative journey. In accompanying Dante, Virgil provides a constant source of dialogue, beckoning, guiding, instructing, cajoling and, at times, admonishing the younger poet, and becoming, as the story progresses, a beloved companion.

Rauschenberg later described the relationship between the medieval poet and the contemporary artist, himself, as one of equals in dialogue: "Dante was sought and completed to have the adventure of what, and if, I could apply my abstract sensibility to a classical restrictive assignment," he wrote to Krauss. "A one-on-one handling and no embarrassment to either. Illustration with compulsive respect."[42] In this striking image, Rauschenberg resurrects the long-dead poet, holding him in the present—he is "sought," demands respect, is capable of embarrassment. The intimacy with Dante that Rauschenberg cultivated may help explain the degree of visceral frustration, even anger, he sometimes felt toward the poet. He described how "the natural interruptions of living in New York, plus my impatience with the morality in Dante, which I didn't agree with, forced me into isolation."[43] Rauschenberg's response to reading Cantos XIV and XV, in which Dante and Virgil encounter the Sodomites in Hell, among whom Virgil discovers his old and beloved teacher Brunetto Latini, was particularly fierce, taking on a sense of personal affront, of disappointment with a friend: "His morality I had to treat objectively—the self-righteousness, the self-appointed conscience imposing guilt on old friends. He was the author, the hero, and the man who made the world described. He ran into his teacher, and couldn't imagine what he was doing in hell: It might not have bothered Dante, but it bothered me."[44] In the drawing that Rauschenberg ultimately made for Canto XIV, he alluded to the punishment in Hell for Sodomites, who must wander eternally on burning sands, by outlining his own foot on the sheet of paper, its scale dominating the page and its indexical self-reference manifest.

Perhaps it was the way that Dante wove together classical and Christian symbolism, contemporary politics and events, and meditations on the public sphere and inner life that allowed Rauschenberg to recognize him as a kindred spirit, if an infuriating one at times—to see in his writing an uncanny precedent for the leveling of symbolic orders high and low, learned and vernacular, that drove so much of the artist's own work. "A pair of socks," Rauschenberg had declared in speaking of his Combines, "is no less suitable to make a painting with than wood, nails, turpentine, oil and fabric."[45] Rauschenberg's choices of contemporary analogues for images and figures present in Dante's text were deeply considered, creating layers of allusion in the relationship between the two. Marginal notes sometimes appear in the artist's dog-eared paperback copy of the Ciardi translation, now in the archives of the Robert Rauschenberg Foundation (figs. 6, 7); for instance, the first page of Canto XII, in which the Centaurs attack the poets, is marked with the words "Centar" and "car [½] vs. man [½]," a substitution of a modern conveyance for an ancient one that ultimately appeared in the corresponding drawing as a fleet of race cars circling the sinners they guard. The image Rauschenberg most frequently used for Dante, which appears for the first time in Canto II, was that of a middle-aged man with a towel draped around his waist, taken from an advertisement in *Sports Illustrated* for golf clubs that could fit players of all sizes (fig. 8). In the original ad, several figures wearing towels are lined up against a ruled background. Rauschenberg later said that it had appealed to him because it was "the most neutral popular image I could find on that scale."[46] He confessed that he panicked when the ad stopped running in the magazine until he found back issues via a wholesaler in New Jersey.[47] When Dante and Virgil are shown together, the travelers often assume a range of contemporary guises for men on the move—a duo of ski racers, runners, scuba divers, motorcyclists, and astronauts. Sometimes the pair's journey is marked only by a double trail of footprints, shoe prints, or legs. Wit is frequent: Virgil's role as superego to the younger Dante is evoked by positioning Virgil as umpire to Dante's baseball player (Canto XXIX) and as an astronaut exhorting Dante's towel-draped everyman from space (Canto XX). George Washington, of Delaware River fame, stands in for Charon of Greek mythology, who ferries the poets across the river Acheron at the border of Hell (Canto III).[48]

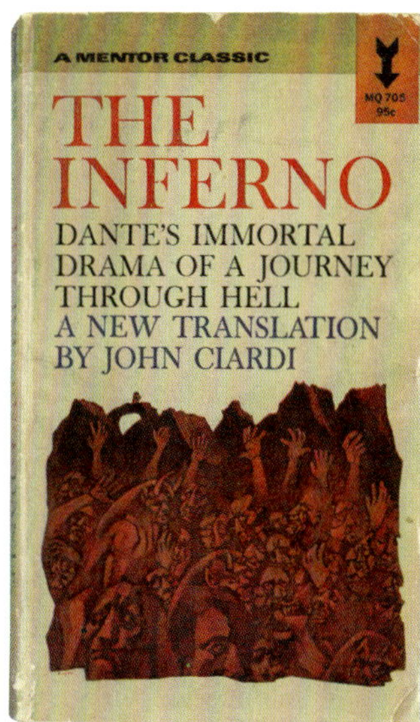

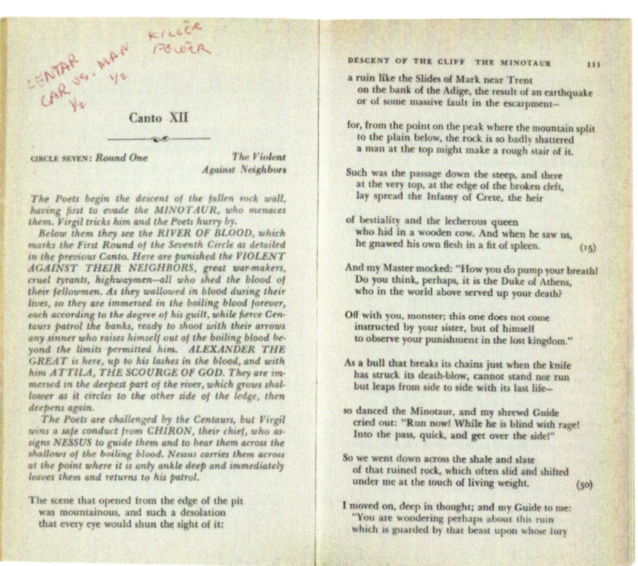

CENTAR
CAR VS. MAN
½ ½
KILLER POWER

Canto XII

CIRCLE SEVEN: *Round One* — *The Violent Against Neighbors*

The Poets begin the descent of the fallen rock wall, having first to evade the MINOTAUR, who menaces them. Virgil tricks him and the Poets hurry by.

Below them they see the RIVER OF BLOOD, which marks the First Round of the Seventh Circle as detailed in the previous Canto. Here are punished the VIOLENT AGAINST THEIR NEIGHBORS, great war-makers, cruel tyrants, highwaymen—all who shed the blood of their fellowmen. As they wallowed in blood during their lives, so they are immersed in the boiling blood forever, each according to the degree of his guilt, while fierce Centaurs patrol the banks, ready to shoot with their arrows any sinner who raises himself out of the boiling blood beyond the limits permitted him. ALEXANDER THE GREAT is here, up to his lashes in the blood, and with him ATTILA, THE SCOURGE OF GOD. They are immersed in the deepest part of the river, which grows shallower as it circles to the other side of the ledge, then deepens again.

The Poets are challenged by the Centaurs, but Virgil wins a safe conduct from CHIRON, their chief, who assigns NESSUS to guide them and to bear them across the shallows of the boiling blood. Nessus carries them across at the point where it is only ankle deep and immediately leaves them and returns to his patrol.

The scene that opened from the edge of the pit
was mountainous, and such a desolation
that every eye would shun the sight of it:

DESCENT OF THE CLIFF THE MINOTAUR 111

a ruin like the Slides of Mark near Trent
on the bank of the Adige, the result of an earthquake
or of some massive fault in the escarpment—

for, from the point on the peak where the mountain split
to the plain below, the rock is so badly shattered
a man at the top might make a rough stair of it.

Such was the passage down the steep, and there
at the very top, at the edge of the broken cleft,
lay spread the Infamy of Crete, the heir

of bestiality and the lecherous queen
who hid in a wooden cow. And when he saw us,
he gnawed his own flesh in a fit of spleen.

And my Master mocked: "How you do pump your breath!
Do you think, perhaps, it is the Duke of Athens,
who in the world above served up your death?

Off with you, monster; this one does not come
instructed by your sister, but of himself
to observe your punishment in the lost kingdom."

As a bull that breaks its chains just when the knife
has struck its death-blow, cannot stand nor run
but leaps from side to side with its last life—

so danced the Minotaur, and my shrewd Guide
cried out: "Run now! While he is blind with rage!
Into the pass, quick, and get over the side!"

So we went down across the shale and slate
of that ruined rock, which often slid and shifted
under me at the touch of living weight.

I moved on, deep in thought; and my Guide to me:
"You are wondering perhaps about this ruin
which is guarded by that beast upon whose fury

6, 7. Cover and interior spread of Rauschenberg's copy of Dante's *Inferno*. *The Inferno: Dante's Immortal Drama of a Journey through Hell*, trans. John Ciardi (New Brunswick, N.J.: Rutgers University Press, 1954). Robert Rauschenberg Foundation, New York

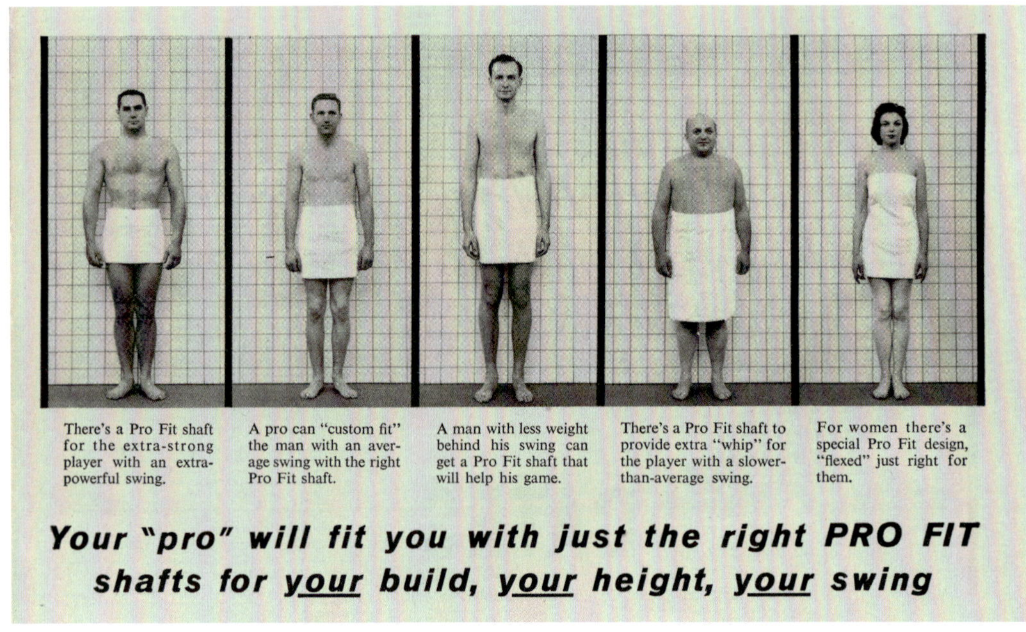

8. Detail from "True Temper Pro Fit" advertisement in *Sports Illustrated*, May 19, 1958, pp. 8–9

Rauschenberg's work on the later cantos, which he saw as "build[ing] up in intensity" with the increasing violence and chaos witnessed by Dante and Virgil as they descend into the lower circles of Hell, coincided with the increasingly fraught presidential election contest between John F. Kennedy and Richard Nixon in 1960; allusions to contemporary events grow more pointed in the later drawings.[49] In Canto XII, Dante and Virgil visit the seventh circle of Hell and encounter those who are "violent against their neighbors, great war-makers, cruel tyrants, highwaymen—those who shed the blood of their fellowmen."[50] Rauschenberg reveals his own sympathies, presenting Dante as Kennedy and Virgil as the respected elder Democratic leader Adlai Stevenson, "the positive image of a politician"[51] in Rauschenberg's telling, while banishing Nixon to the river of boiling blood below. "If you feel strongly, it's going to show.... The one thing that has been consistent about my work is that there is an attempt to use the very last minute in my life and the particular location as the source of energy and inspiration," he commented, all the while rejecting the idea of making more overtly exhortative artwork such as Pablo Picasso's famous *Guernica*.[52]

"Only the key images are to be read explicitly," Dore Ashton pointed out.[53] They appear against fields of overlaid washes that conjure forces of movement, foregrounding the nature of an epic as a journey through time and space. Transferred images occur in different orientations, flopped in reverse, sometimes right side up, sometimes upside down, seeming to spin and turn within an aqueous space. Rauschenberg often created ruled divisions on the page that suggest temporal sequence in the style of comic books, photo-stories, Renaissance predellas, or, as Ashton put it, "film strips sliding downward."[54] Sometimes the artist added elements that suggest motion—arrows, dotted lines, a bird in flight. The paper supports appear as perceptive screens, registering the rich panoply of smells, sounds, and sensations evoked in Dante's verses. Noise, for example, is rendered as staccato strokes of graphite (Cantos III and VI), the poets' entrance into a green meadow as a vision with a frame, washed in green (Canto IV), a putrid odor as a seeping ochre wash (Canto XVI).[55] The result, Rauschenberg wrote in his failed Guggenheim application, "seems to indicate a large and complex 'view' or 'scene,' containing implications of activity and changes of movement from the literal to figurative, from the general to the specific."[56]

In his own writing, Ciardi insisted that translation was the "wrong word" when applied to poetry; the idea of "transposition" was more apt. "When the violin repeats what the piano has just played," he explained, "it cannot make the same sounds, it cannot form identical notes, and it can only approximate the same chords. It can, however, produce recognizably the same air, the same 'music.' … It is the music one must go for, not the notes."[57] Rauschenberg went for the music.

He conceived the translation from poetry to drawing as a dialogue between two voices; the pains with which "Dante was sought" attest to that. As Rauschenberg later stressed in his notes to Krauss, the act of sustained engagement was also one of self-construction: "Attempting Dante was a private exercise in my growth and self-exploration to face my weaknesses. A test. By doing it I had equal opportunity to alienate or to ally."[58] In this recounting, one senses that with the Dante project Rauschenberg was pushing back against his own insecurities around his upbringing, his age, his difficulty reading, his abstract sensibility, his acceptance by the art world, and his sexuality. The finished drawings have been rightfully read as giving veiled commentary on gay love.[59] Yet they also address companionate affection, the frictious ties of rivals, the bond between ruler and subject, and the lingering tethers between the dead and the living. As a whole, the series offers a broad meditation on myriad forces of power—those of desire, politics, and culture included—and the way that they become manifest in an individual's life. It is telling that for this artist who understood artwork as an encounter "with something already in existence,"[60] the test was structured via a chain of collaborations and dialogues stretching over time: in the encounters between himself and Dante, between Dante and Virgil long before that, and with Ciardi, Sonnabend, and Ashton, each a testament to the defining forces one being can exert on another—each encounter an "opportunity to alienate or ally."

Notes

1. Rauschenberg, in Rosalind Krauss, "Perpetual Inventory," 1997, in Branden W. Joseph, ed., *Robert Rauschenberg*, October Files 4 (Cambridge, Mass.: The MIT Press, 2002), p. 103. In an unpublished and undated interview with Calvin Tomkins conducted in preparation for Tomkins's book *Off the Wall: A Portrait of Robert Rauschenberg* (New York: Picador, 1980), Rauschenberg says, similarly, "I wanted to make more drawings." Calvin Tomkins Papers, IV.C.19, The Museum of Modern Art Archives, New York.

2. Rauschenberg, in Krauss, "Perpetual Inventory," p. 103.

3. Rauschenberg, in Dorothy Gees Seckler, "The Artist Speaks: Robert Rauschenberg," *Art in America* 54, no. 3 (May–June 1966): 84.

4. Rauschenberg, in Dorothy Gees Seckler, "Oral history interview with Robert Rauschenberg," December 21, 1965, n.p. Archives of American Art, Smithsonian Institution. Available online at www.aaa.si.edu/collections/interviews/oralhistory-interview-robert-rauschenberg-12870 (accessed July 2016).

5. Rauschenberg suggests this in conversation with Tomkins. Tomkins, IV.C.19, The Museum of Modern Art Archives.

6. Rauschenberg, in ibid.

7. Rauschenberg, in ibid. It remains unclear which of the thirty-four drawings were done in New York, and which in Florida. In this quotation, Rauschenberg suggests that "the last half" were made in Florida. In another passage in this interview, he implies that he was still in New York when he took up the Sodomites passages of Cantos XIV and XV: "Once I started in on Dante, I found the natural interruptions of living in New York, plus my impatience with the morality in Dante, which I didn't agree with, forced me into isolation.... He ran into his teacher, and couldn't imagine what he was doing in hell. It might not have bothered Dante, but it bothered me.... Anyway I had to get out of New York."

8. Stuart Preston, "Cards of Identity: Dante Revisited," *New York Times*, December 11, 1960.

9. See Dore Ashton, *Thirty-Four Drawings for Dante's Inferno* (New York: Harry N. Abrams, 1964), p. 3; Roberta Smith, "Art: Drawings by Robert Rauschenberg, 1958–68," *New York Times*, October 31, 1986; and Roni Feinstein, "Random Order: The First Fifteen Years of Robert Rauschenberg's Art, 1949–1964," PhD diss., New York University, 1990, p. 351.

10. Branden Joseph, "Split Screens," in *Random Order: Robert Rauschenberg and the Neo-Avant-Garde* (Cambridge, Mass.: The MIT Press, 2003), p. 177.

11. Rauschenberg, in Tomkins, IV.C.19, The Museum of Modern Art Archives.

12. Ibid. Tomkins notes, "In Cuba, he hit on the rubbing technique, doing it first dry, using comic strips from newspapers and magazines. Later he found it was easier to wet the paper first with turpentine. Recently he has refined the process even further, using lighter fluid and an empty ballpoint pen."

13. Krauss, "Perpetual Inventory," p. 95.

14. Hal Foster develops a theory of Pop art in *The First Pop Age: Painting and Subjectivity in the Art of Hamilton, Lichtenstein, Warhol, Richter, and Ruscha* (Princeton, N.J.: Princeton University Press, 2014).

15. Krauss, "Perpetual Inventory," p. 97.

16. Rauschenberg, in ibid.

17. Rauschenberg notes this in several interviews, including in Barbara Rose, *An Interview with Robert Rauschenberg* (New York: Vintage Books, 1987), p. 100, and in his unpublished interview with Tomkins. Tomkins, IV.C.19, The Museum of Modern Art Archives.

18. Rauschenberg, Oral History Program, interview with Joachim Pissarro, April 20, 2006, p. 6. The Museum of Modern Art Archives.

19. This description appears on Rauschenberg's *Autobiography* (1968), a lithographic print in the collection of The Museum of Modern Art.

20. Tomkins, *Off the Wall*, p. 133.

21. Annie Cohen-Solal, *Leo and His Circle: The Life of Leo Castelli*, trans. Mark Polizzotti with the author (New York: Alfred A. Knopf, 2010), p. 152.

22. Nina Sundell, in Cohen-Solal, *Leo and His Circle*, p. 152.

23. Edward M. Cifelli, *John Ciardi: A Biography* (Fayetteville: University of Arkansas Press, 1997), pp. 192–93.

24. Dudley Fitts, "Translated into American," *New York Times*, July 4, 1954.

25. Dante Alighieri, *The Divine Comedy 1: Hell*, trans. Dorothy L. Sayers (London: Penguin Books, 1950), p. 100.

26. Dante Alighieri, *The Divine Comedy: The Inferno, The Purgatorio, and The Paradiso*, trans. John Ciardi (New York: New American Library, 2003), p. 49.

27. Rauschenberg, in Rose, *An Interview with Robert Rauschenberg*, p. 100.

28. Ciardi, footnote in Dante, *The Divine Comedy: The Inferno, The Purgatorio, and The Paradiso*, p. 52.

29. Clive James, introduction to *The Divine Comedy*, by Dante Alighieri, trans. James (London: Picador, 2013), p. xxi.

30. Rauschenberg, in Tomkins, IV.C.19, The Museum of Modern Art Archives.

31. Rauschenberg, in Seckler, "The Artist Speaks," p. 84.

32. Tomkins, IV.C.19, The Museum of Modern Art Archives. Rauschenberg is quoted as saying, "The concept of an artist isolating his or her favorite event can pull a particular passage into popular distortion."

33. Rauschenberg, in Krauss, "Perpetual Inventory," p. 103. Rauschenberg put it another way to Tomkins: "If the most important thing on the page took only three words, I would make it a proportionate size." Tomkins, IV.C.19, The Museum of Modern Art Archives.

34. Michael Sonnabend, in an unpublished interview with Billy Klüver and Julie Martin, 1991. Made available to the author by Martin.

35. Rauschenberg, in Graham Smith, "'Visibile Parlare': Rauschenberg's Drawings for Dante's *Inferno*," *Word and Image* 32, no. 1 (January–March 2016): 84.

36. Sonnabend, interview with Klüver and Martin, 1991.

37. Julie Martin's recollection, as recounted by Robert Whitman in an interview with Alessandra Nicifero, Robert Rauschenberg Oral History Project (November 20, 2014), Robert Rauschenberg Foundation, New York, p. 36. Available online at http://www.rauschenbergfoundation.org/artist/oral-history/robert-whitman (accessed February 2017); Joan Young and Susan Davidson, "Chronology," in Walter Hopps and Susan Davidson, eds., *Robert Rauschenberg: A Retrospective*, exh. cat. (New York: Solomon R. Guggenheim Museum, 1997), p. 556.

38. Sonnabend, interview with Klüver and Martin, 1991.

39. Ashton, "The Collaboration Wheel: A Comment on Robert Rauschenberg's Comment on Dante," *Arts and Architecture* 80, no. 2 (December 1963): 37.

40. William Harris, "The Sin of Silent Reading," n.d. Available online at community.middlebury.edu/~harris/LatinBackground/SilentReading.html (accessed January 2017). Roman villas had reading rooms so that the master of the house might read without disturbing the rest of the family. See also Barbara Reynolds, introduction to *Dante: The Poet, the Political Thinker, the Man* (London: I. B. Tauris, 2006), pp. xii–xiii.

41. Reynolds, introduction to *Dante*, p. xii.

42. Rauschenberg, in Krauss, "Perpetual Inventory," p. 102.

43. Rauschenberg, in Tomkins, IV.C.19, The Museum of Modern Art Archives.

44. Ibid. Martin Gayford also recalls Rauschenberg's distress at Dante's moralizing: "He singled out the episode in Canto XV when the poet encounters his old teacher Brunetto Latini among the sodomites, condemned to jog eternally across the burning sands of Hell. '*Siete voi qui, ser Brunetto?*' Dante exclaims in surprise. Or, as Rauschenberg freely paraphrased, 'What a surprise seeing you here! I'm so sorry.' But he immediately protested, 'Dante wrote the fucking thing!'" Gayford, "The World in His Hands," *Art Quarterly*, Winter 2016, 16.

45. Rauschenberg, statement in Dorothy C. Miller, *Sixteen Americans*, exh. cat. (New York: The Museum of Modern Art, 1959), p. 58.

46. Rauschenberg, in Tomkins, IV.C.19, The Museum of Modern Art Archives.

47. Ibid.

48. Smith, "'Visibile Parlare,'" p. 79.

49. See Ed Krčma, "To Use the Very Last Minute in My Life: The Dante Drawings and the Classical Past," in Leah Dickerman and Achim Borchardt-Hume, *Robert Rauschenberg*, exh. cat. (New York: The Museum of Modern Art, 2016), pp. 162–69.

50. Dante, *The Divine Comedy*, trans. Ciardi, p. 96.

51. Rauschenberg, in Tomkins, IV.C.19, The Museum of Modern Art Archives.

52. Rauschenberg, in Seckler, "The Artist Speaks," p. 84.

53. Ashton, *Thirty-Four Drawings for Dante's Inferno*, p. 4.

54. Ibid.

55. Ibid.

56. Rauschenberg, application to the John Simon Guggenheim Memorial Foundation, 1958. Robert Rauschenberg Foundation Archives, New York.

57. Ciardi, in Cifelli, *John Ciardi*, p. 189.

58. Rauschenberg, in Krauss, "Perpetual Inventory," p. 103.

59. See Laura Auricchio, "Lifting the Veil: Rauschenberg's *Thirty-Four Drawings for Dante's Inferno* and the Commercial Homoerotic Imagery of 1950s America," in Thomas Foster, Carol Siegel, and Ellen E. Berry, eds., *The Gay '90s: Disciplinary and Interdisciplinary Formations in Queer Studies* (New York: New York University Press, 1997), pp. 119–54.

60. Rauschenberg, in Seckler, "The Artist Speaks," p. 84.

Harrowing
a short history of Hell

Kevin Young

A goat with a tire around its belly. A dirty bed on a wall. A man falling through space. A dead president. An abandoned, stuffed bald eagle. In a certain light, Robert Rauschenberg's famed Combine paintings and artworks delineate the stuff of Hell. *A canvas completely, almost completely, red.*

✶

In my high school in Kansas, we had a class called Humanities. It was great, one of those holdovers from the 1970s in which we studied not a specific area of art but all arts, team-taught of course in a large room that felt like a rehearsal space, with moveable chairs but no desks. The teachers too were holdovers, severe and inspiring in turn. I remember less in terms of specific artworks we looked at than the general ethos of adventure and connection, with two exceptions: Leonard Bernstein's *Mass* for John F. Kennedy (who centers one of Rauschenberg's key works) and the opening of the Kennedy Center; and Dante's *Inferno* in the John Ciardi translation, the very one that Rauschenberg encountered while he was making his drawings. Later, while we were in class, the space shuttle *Challenger* exploded while other classes at school were watching live—we weren't—and the music teacher of the team burst into the room, announcing the Dantean tragedy. It took time for it all to sink in.

✶

Upon first reading the *Inferno*, I immediately took to its epic achievement built on a kind of revenge fantasy. Dante makes high art of our low impulses: vengeance, fate, sorrow, swooning, shame, deeply pained pity, feigned sympathy. It can feel a lot like high school.

✶

Hell, a working definition: *n.*, a place one does not wish to be yet remains far longer than one can stand or imagine.

✶

Rereading Dante delivers different pleasures and pains. That first time at Topeka West, the poem felt quite present—for among its sorrow is also a kind of cosmic rationale, a reasoning that Dante the naïf can only glimpse at times. These days it is the politics of the *Inferno* that seem awfully relevant; it is a deeply political poem. One friend says that Dante is often petty, and this is true—this is another way of saying the poem is partisan, placing in deepest Hell those who betrayed Dante or his causes. It seems instructive: Hell is personal.

✶

Hell, a short history: Dante. Bosch. Milton. Blake. Rimbaud. In the West, where it most exists as an idea, Hell only accelerates across the twentieth century: *The Waste Land*; Pound's Hell Cantos, taking place during the Great War, then the Hell of Pisan Cantos after the Second World War, which pictures paradise, always unfinished. H.D.'s *Trilogy*. Sartre. Ginsberg's *Howl*. Baraka's *System of Dante's Hell*. Robert Pinsky's grand translation. Seamus Heaney's translation of the first canto. Robert Johnson's "Me and the Devil Blues" as covered by the late Gil Scott-Heron: harrowing.

✶

The Harrowing of Hell means the opposite of how it may sound: it is the apocryphal, Apostles' Creed account of Jesus' descent to Hell and saving those infants and innocents found in Limbo. Such a descent to the underworld to rescue someone has been with us at least since the Greeks; Dante's brilliance throughout the *Inferno* especially is to incorporate the whole of Western mythology, Greek and especially Roman myth. The poem is awfully pagan, which is to say, it feels modern and ancient at once.

Rauschenberg's drawings for Dante's *Inferno* manage much the same.

✶

Heaney's translation seems to me the most perfect English rendering of the famed opening stanza of the *Inferno*:

> *In the middle of the journey of our life*
> *I found myself astray in a dark wood*
> *where the straight road had been lost sight of.*

Saying "our life" instead of *mine*; the passive voice of the last lines and the slant rhyme: it is hard to resolve the problems, the passions, of Dante, much less the prosody. Heaney, my onetime teacher, is teaching us all here. I once asked him a few years after I studied with him about the translations and did he ever consider doing all of the *Inferno*? We were then, at that moment, at the bottom of a drained swimming pool, watching my roommate perform an adaptation of Heaney's translated *Sweeney Astray*, the old Irish poem. We had climbed down the pool's ladder to sit and watch his beloved words said by my beloved friend. Descent means rising on the other side.

Heaney answered that he wasn't prepared to give over a decade to it, at least—and I saw then that the crossroads that Dante and Heaney described to me were real. We must pick, though often "the straight road had been lost sight of."

✶

I thought a lot about "the middle" after that. My poetic work was just beginning, yet I had already written most of what would become my first book, in a fever it felt—by instinct and discipline—and it was suddenly being published. What was next? I turned inward—going from poems about my parents' and grandparents' Louisiana, and an often imagined state, to poems about growing up in the middle of the country. I hoped I could write that elusive thing, a personal epic, mostly built on memory. I thought of the poems as making up a trilogy—since Dante, I've always loved superstructures—made explicit as "circles" even.

But lyrics are hard, epics even harder, and a lyric epic almost impossible. Luckily I didn't publish it in that form, though certain poems have poked their heads up into other works. Instead, I wrote a lyric epic that wasn't dependent on memory, about the late painter Jean-Michel Basquiat, who painted his own thorny halos and crooked crowns.

Our failures, Hell teaches us, are instructive too.

✶

I learned just last week that Heaney's translation of book six of Virgil's *Aeneid* will soon appear posthumously, giving Heaney's cast to Dante's guide. His powerful translation of Dante's third canto, "The Crossing," already concludes *Seeing Things* with an account of Charon the ferryman in honor of his late father. Having lost my father, and now Heaney, I must say that sometimes, capturing even one moment of the afterlife or the underworld may be enough.

✶

The orality of Dante's poem we mostly lose in English. The terza rima or perpetual rhyme scheme he uses is near impossible in our tongue. That's why I think the best approximation of the sound of Dante, its vernacular, repetitive, interlocking rhyme, may be the blues. The blues also believe that the Devil is no abstraction. You say, *the dark wood*; I say, *I went down to the crossroads* and *There's a Hellhound on my trail*.

✶

Can Rauschenberg be said to exhibit, not the blues, but the reds? That, and yellow, crawl through the greys of his Dante drawings: a blood-red footprint; a giant spider; Satan's left eye. The *Inferno's* final canto, and Rauschenberg's accompanying drawing, drew me into a different direction than I might—my temptation was not to end, as Dante does, with stars, but with a cleansing rain. But yes, stars; and moreover, I had to get that Devil's eye in there, its disturbing triple heads like Cerberus, who Virgil keeps at bay with a mere word. The hounds of Hell; *A Hellhound on My Trail*: the way Hell hounds us.

✶

There is another African American folk tradition in which the Devil is not a threat but a trickster. Zora Neale Hurston writes powerfully of this in *Mules and Men*—Lucifer rather than Satan, devilish rather than demonic. Again, we witness the European overidentification of blackness with evil being reclaimed by black people themselves. Dante, his visage a symbolic scowl, mostly avoids this.

Hell, too, is often painted by the black artist or folk preacher as here and now, whether Rastafarian Babylon or Hurston's West Hell. Both are just next door, and coming ever closer.

✶

Scott-Heron's "Me and the Devil Blues" was released on his final album, *I'm New Here*, his first studio recording in well over a decade. A year later he was dead. That is, unless you believe, as he sounds on the recording, he was already gone—his voice is haunting, and haunted, not so much posthumous as pre-posthumous—taken from us by things worse than death. *If you've got to pay for things you've done wrong, I've got a big bill coming*, he says in one of the many interview interludes included as interstitial tracks. That is Hell's lesson, and Rauschenberg's revelation, found in another of Scott-Heron's last songs: *No matter how far wrong you've gone, you can always turn around*. It's never too late.

✶

The repetition of threes, both in the blues and in Dante, finds its way into the poems you find here by me and Robin Coste Lewis. I am tempted to say they do this in opposite ways: in my sequence *The Dark Wood*, with its tercets and repetition of "the dead"; for Robin, in her section, *Dante Comes to America: 20 January 2017, An Erasure of 17 Cantos from Ciardi's "Inferno" After Robert Rauschenberg*, in which she repeats by eliminating what's there. Robin's erasure also brings to mind one of Rauschenberg's early triumphs, namely, his *Erased de Kooning Drawing*.

I note that neither of us included guides like Dante's Virgil—instead, it's only *The Dark Road pointing us toward the needle's eye*. Yet both of our approaches are ways of removing yet reinforcing the word and the world: in short, charting Hell. Here it is, coming up on your left: *Step lively*.

Canto I. *The Dark Wood*

In my living
    room, the skull
of the coyote

discusses with me
    our pending appointment
with bone—the canine teeth

of time. The middle
    of my life. His grin
is not found

in the smaller antlers
    of the antelope
once found by my father

that also flowers
    from the wall. Down
in the square, trees

bare as bones, their crown
    of leaves shorn. The hounds
of the constables hollering

the lure of light & gas
    in lanterns. Guns. My feet
deep in the mud

of what is called Wood
    or Gardens the government
built just for us. Your mama's

leopard clutch
    rustling with peppermints.
A one-eyed cat.

A wolf in silhouette—
    that whistle. The coyote
in the quiet.

    The hour of our hunger
is his, only longer.

K.Y.

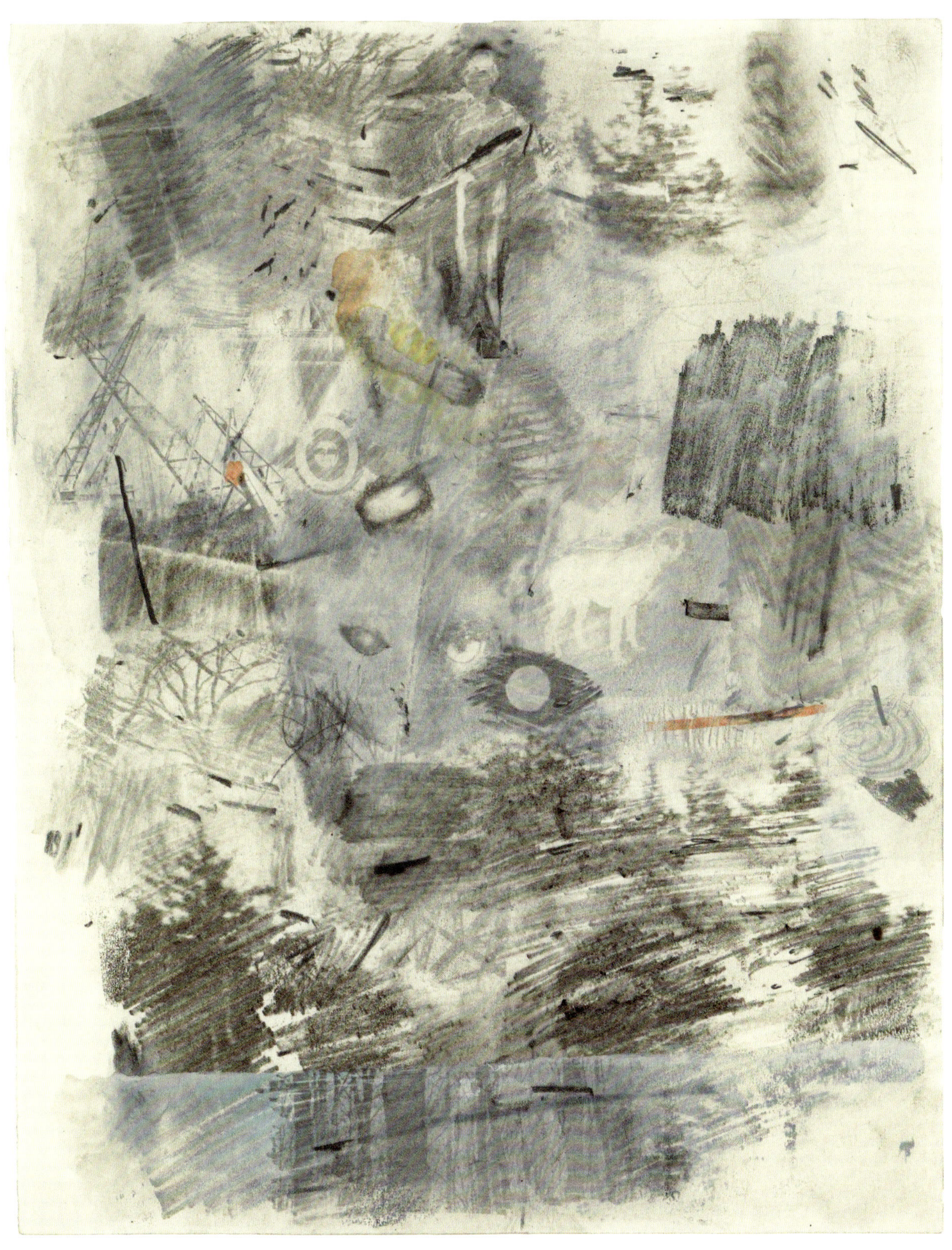

CANTO I: THE DARK WOOD OF ERROR. 1958
Solvent transfer drawing, pencil, gouache, and
colored pencil on paper, 14½ x 11½ in. (36.8 x 29.2 cm)
The Museum of Modern Art, New York. Given anonymously

Canto II. *The Descent*

What will
        become of us?
The blue wash

& the arrows aiming
        us on: No Exit.
No Trespasses

No Breath.
        Are you willing
& able to assist?

asks the Captain.
        Dry docked
& airlocked, the cruel capsule

we barely glimpse
        Earth from.
Ladies & gentlemen,

we cannot move till everyone
        is seated.
We hold each

other awaiting
        the splash of landing—
prepare for impact—

our vessel's crash
        & flush
sounding down in the blue.

The lake of my heart.
        The light departing.
All around us, new

in the briar of after—
        a lone goose, or loon,
low overhead. The white

ring around their necks.
        What was next:
arms raised to reach

the banking birds—
        hands up don't
shoot—or as if we might,

ourselves, take flight.

K.Y.

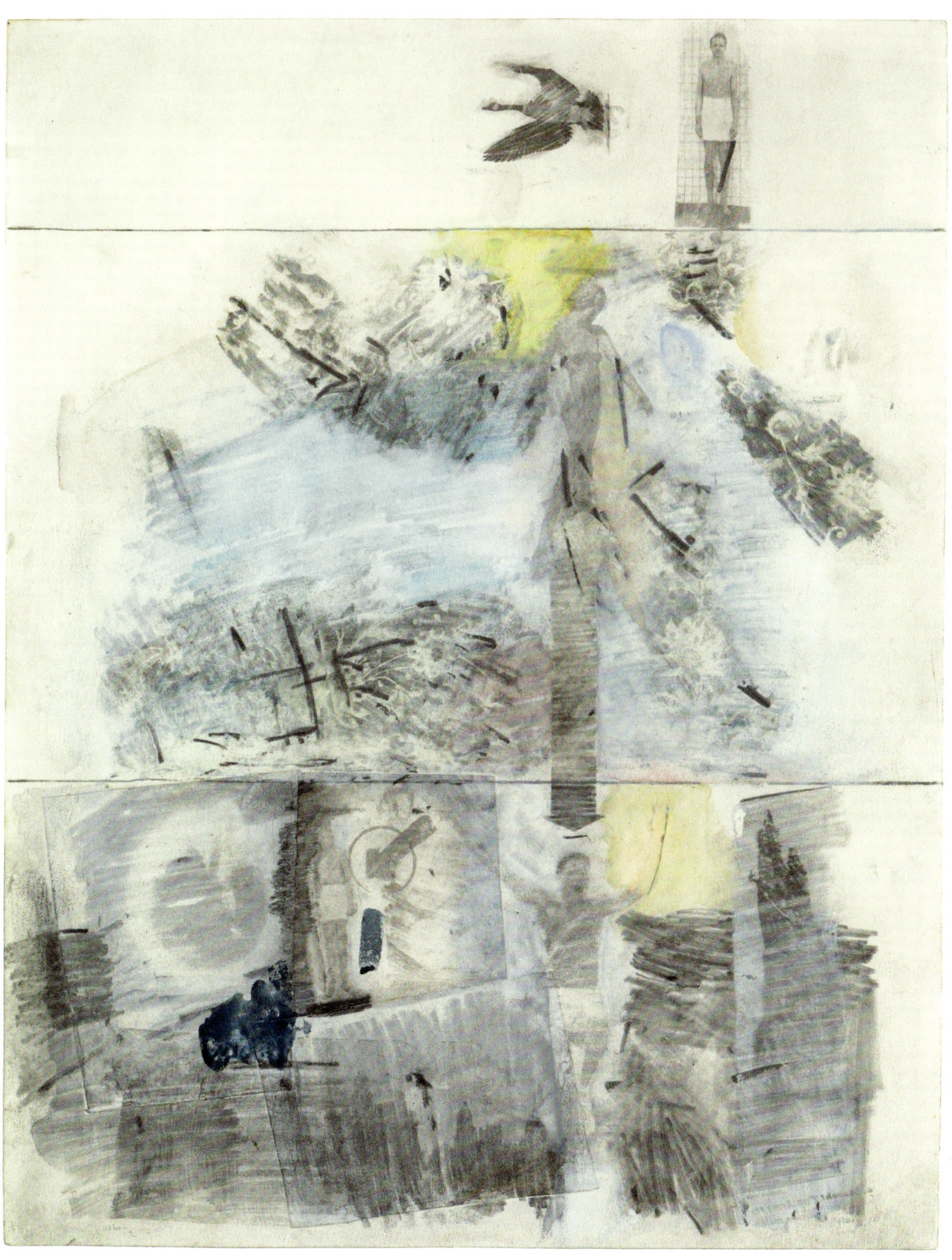

CANTO II: THE DESCENT. 1958
Solvent transfer drawing, pencil, gouache, and colored pencil on cut-and-pasted paper on paper, 14 3/8 x 11 3/8 in. (36.5 x 28.9 cm)
The Museum of Modern Art, New York. Given anonymously

Canto III. *Vestibule (City of Woe)*

Babylon was busy.
        Frisked & let through
we stepped into

Death's waiting room.
        The magazines old
as your mama's—

Time or *Life*
        with the address
ripped off. For safety.

Ebony. The Doctor will
        see you now—will
bill you, will

kneel on your chest
        to stop the bullet
or breath. *Jet*.

Sweet Spirit. Each body only
        what will not be.
Each room an emergency

none yet can see.

K.Y.

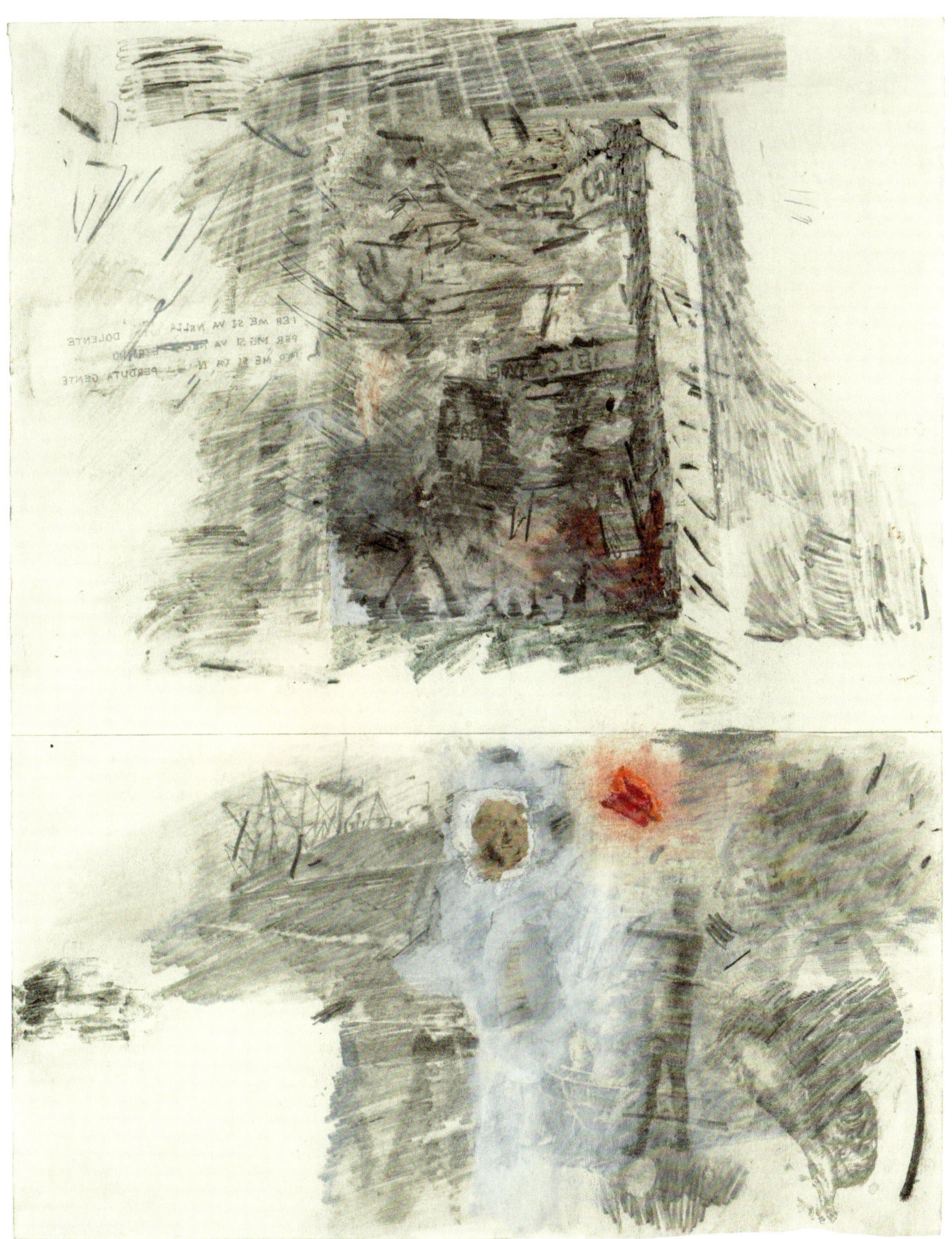

CANTO III: THE VESTIBULE OF HELL, THE OPPORTUNISTS. 1958
Solvent transfer drawing, torn-and-pasted paper, watercolor, and pencil on paper, 14 3/8 x 11 3/8 in. (36.5 x 28.9 cm)
The Museum of Modern Art, New York. Given anonymously

Canto IV. *Limbo (Circle One)*

Skeleton-still.
    We stood. Those
before us who once

Almost believed, arrayed
    like statues, trophies
of the child killed

We couldn't bear
    to dust
or box away.

The dark arch
    to the lost teen's
bedroom, jersey

Now empty, baseball team
    down a man—
out with an injury.

Wild pitch. Passed ball.
    Technical knockout.
Technical foul.

Flagrant two. The flagration
    of the car turned over
he lay dead beside

A good while.
    Dark dye
seeping into the street.

No pop flies. No catch—
    player to be
named later—

No sheet we'll provide—
    Just the blue-tail fly
doornailed, hungry,

Fit to die.

K.Y.

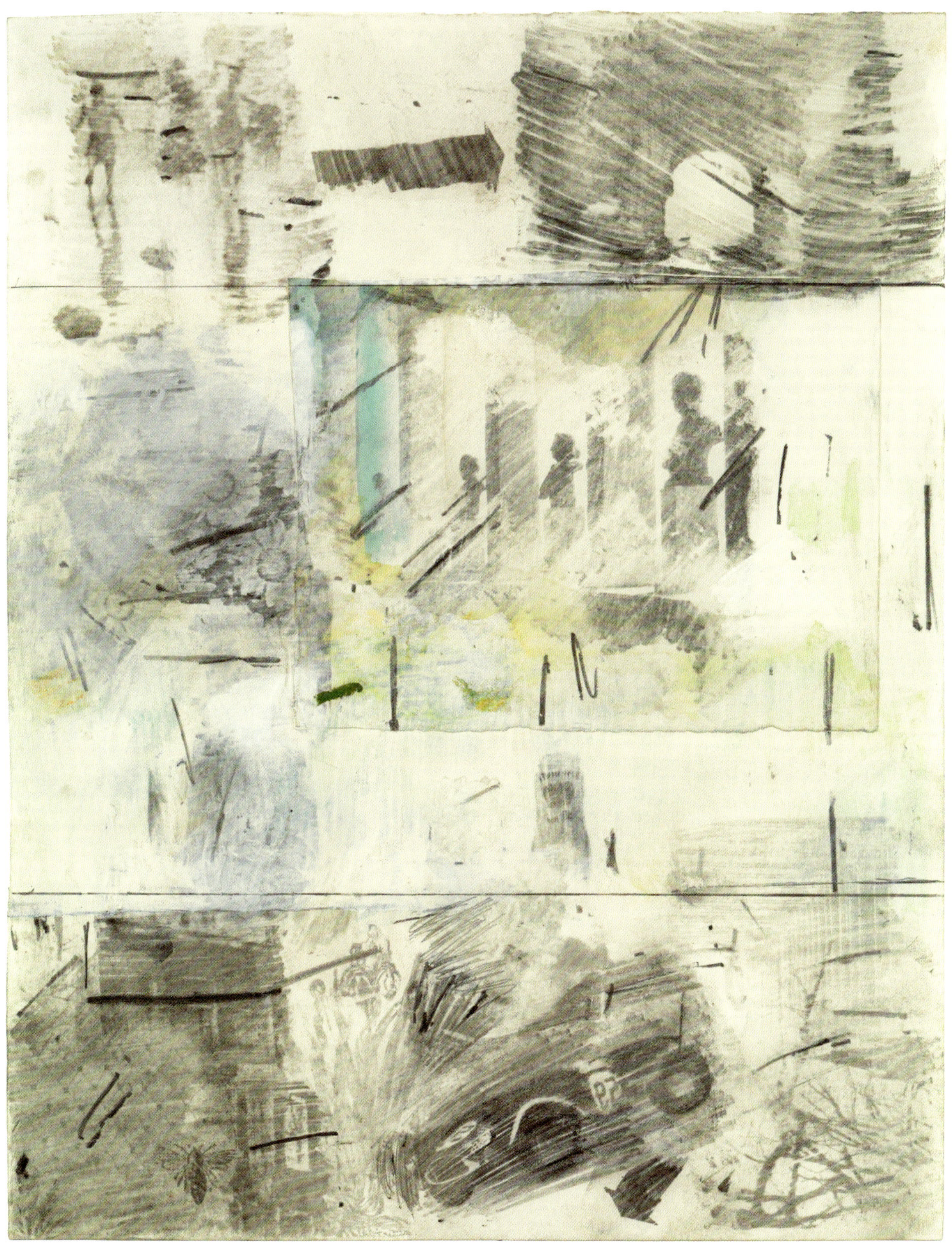

CANTO IV: LIMBO, CIRCLE ONE, THE VIRTUOUS PAGANS. 1958
Solvent transfer drawing, cut-and-pasted paper, pencil, gouache, and watercolor on paper, 14 1/2 x 11 1/2 in. (36.8 x 29.2 cm)
The Museum of Modern Art, New York. Given anonymously

Canto V. *Noli Me Tangere (Circle Two: The Carnal)*

The dead want us
        to want them, lovers
of what isn't there—

or is that us—
        leaning close, infidels
of the world's invisible

unliving long train.
        The dead, wedded
to this world, vow

beneath a veil.
        In the mirror
we meet the dead

each morning—
        shaving, say,
we rake our faces

of yesterday—
        or darken our eyes
in order to leave

out the house. When we smile
        the dead nod back—
when we laugh the dead don't

seem to mind. Tonight
        the lost rise
with the moon above

the mountain, a stone
        rolled back
from the tomb—the body

stolen of its soul—
        the blind world
or whirlwind—

In daylight, see it
        list in the sky
sometimes, the moon—

ghostly eye, great
        unremembered rock,
bare mirror

        where we
cannot breathe.

K.Y.

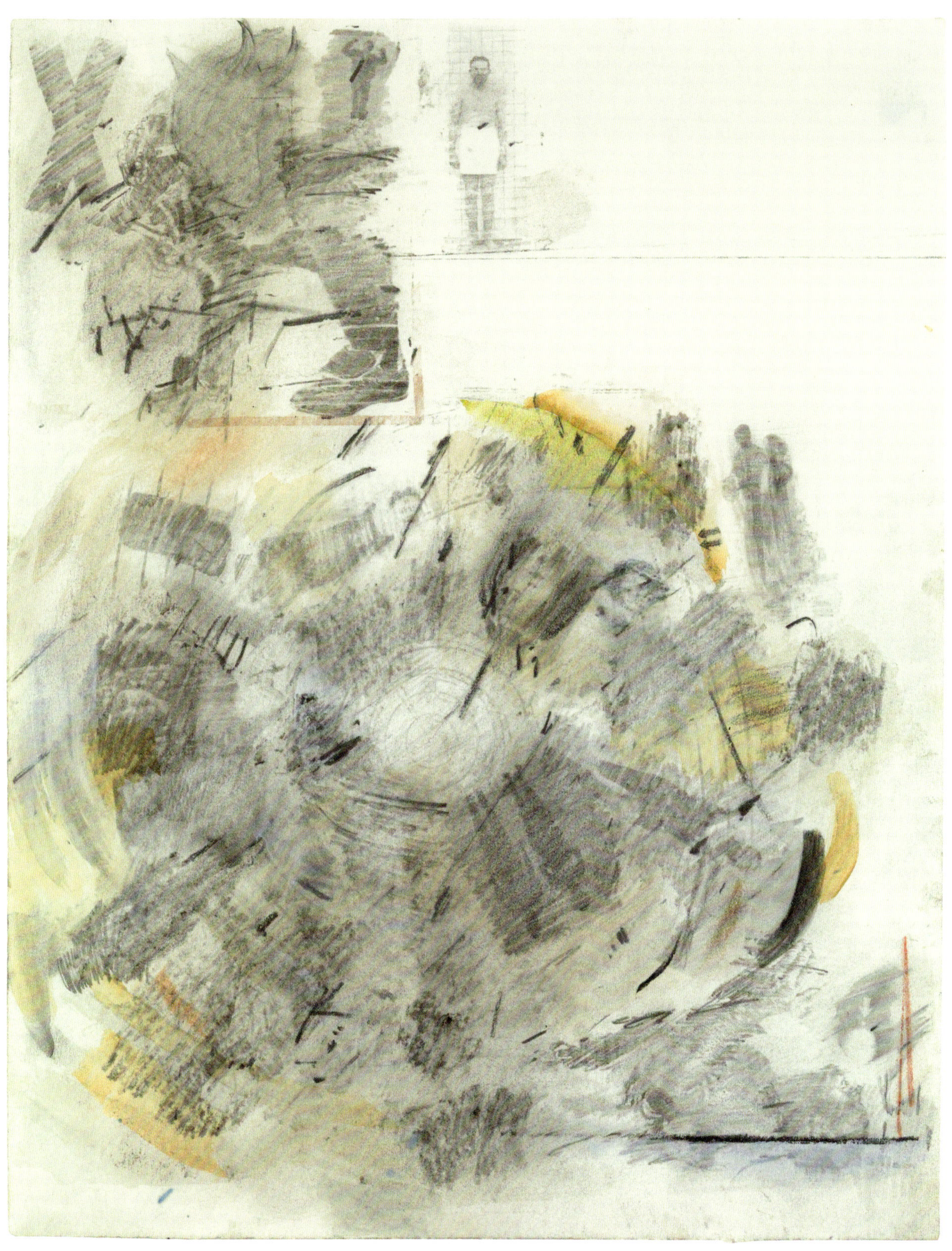

CANTO V: CIRCLE TWO, THE CARNAL. 1958
Solvent transfer drawing, watercolor, pencil, crayon, and gouache on paper, 14 3/8 x 11 1/2 in. (36.5 x 29.2 cm)
The Museum of Modern Art, New York. Given anonymously

Canto VI. *Underworld (Circle Three)*

We are born
        with all our grief
already in us, like teeth,

& time works it out
        of us—our mouths—pain
for a time & then there

grief sits, forever, shiny,
        lucky. Pomegranate. Made
before I was unmade—

If not, the gaps
        where once milkteeth sat,
replaced by these holes

        we hope to eat with—
each supper a reckoning.
K.Y.

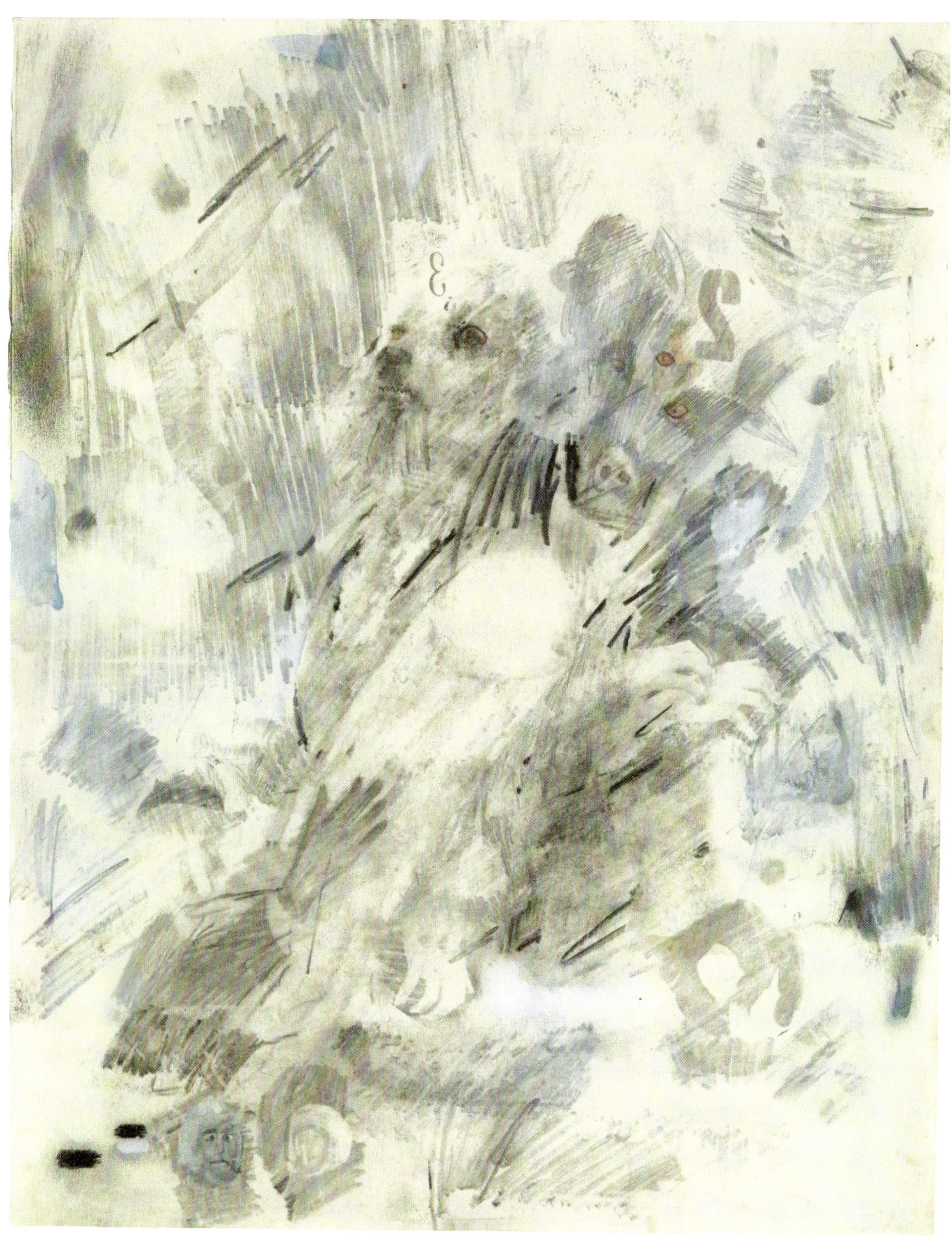

CANTO VI: CIRCLE THREE, THE GLUTTONS. 1958
Solvent transfer drawing, gouache, pencil, and
watercolor on paper, 14 3/8 x 11 1/2 in. (36.5 x 29.2 cm)
The Museum of Modern Art, New York. Given anonymously

Canto VII. *Black Spring (Circles Four & Five)*

I hate the heart—
        how it isn't
ever done, finds

its way forward
        though the head
may not want. We may

have to say Let go
        to those we love,
it's alright to leave—

not permitted to stay—

that very night, absolved,
        tonsured with tubes,
they up

& do. The world apparently
        is hard to fight
free from, rocketing

away from gravity
        & the pear trees
blooming early

before I was even ready
        to believe again
in beauty.

K.Y.

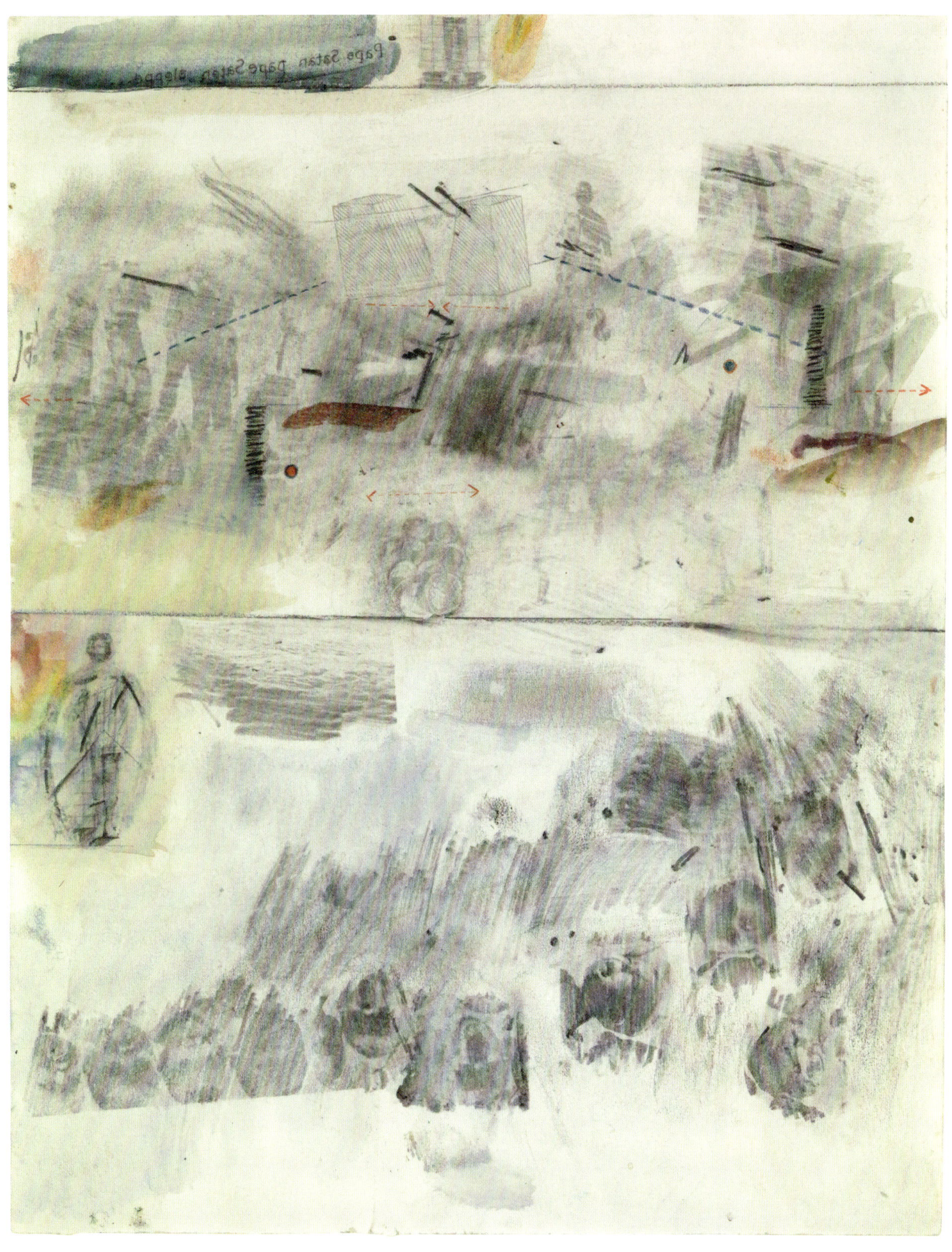

CANTO VII: CIRCLE FOUR, THE HOARDERS AND THE WASTERS;
CIRCLE FIVE, THE WRATHFUL AND THE SULLEN. 1959–60
Solvent transfer drawing, pencil, watercolor, and colored pencil on paper, 14 3/8 x 11 3/8 in. (36.5 x 28.9 cm)
The Museum of Modern Art, New York. Given anonymously

Canto VIII. *Wake of Souls (Circle Five: The Styx)*

The dead don't know
        what to do
with themselves.

Aren't enough,
        our arms—
See them crowd

the river's edge
        eager, or afraid
to cross

this marsh of souls.
        The boat late,
of course, its skeleton

crew of one.
        Infected light.
Sunless tide.

So many. They yearn
        for what
they fear—

Our prayers cheer
        or jeer them along—
the oars enter

        the water
with a moan.

K.Y.

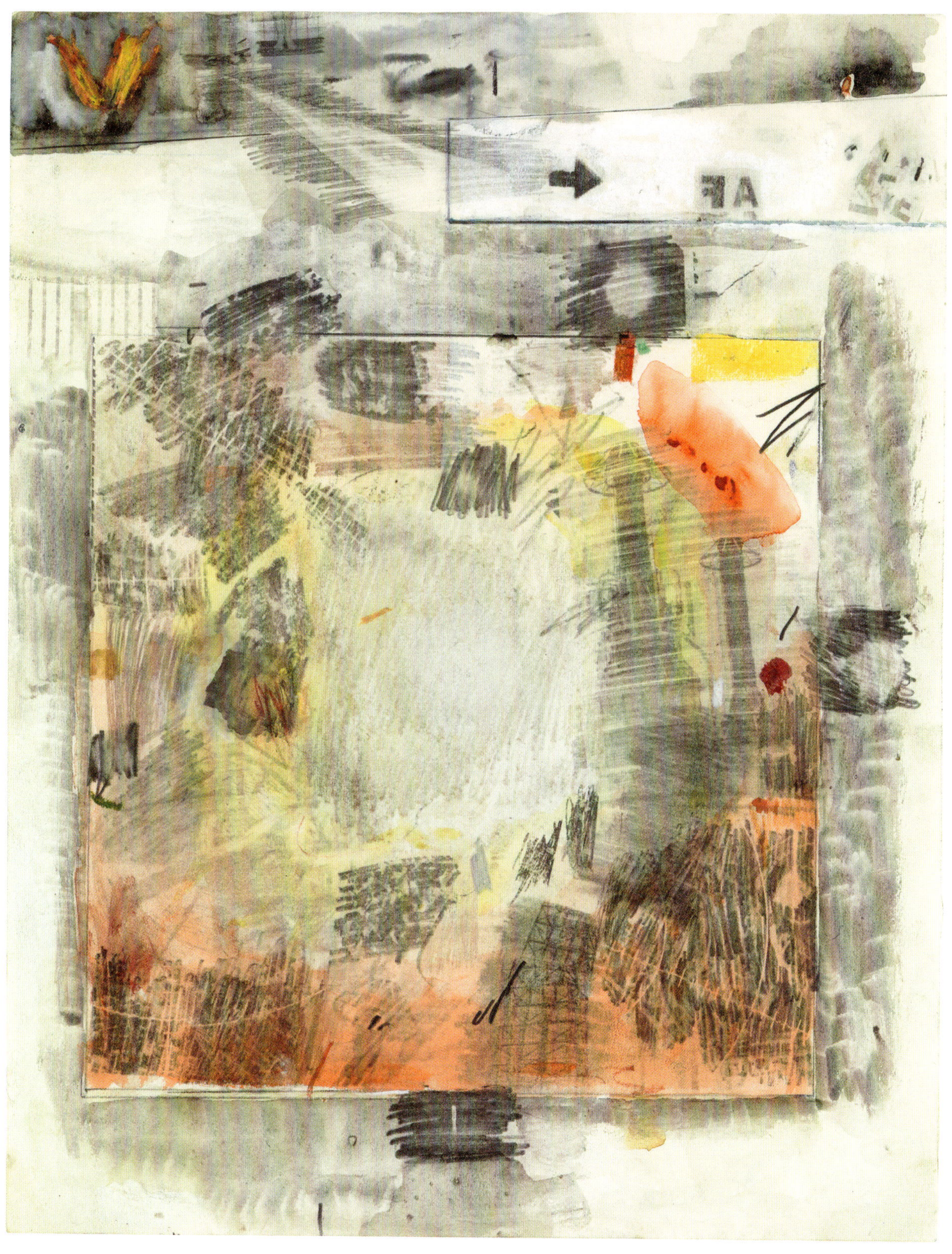

CANTO VIII: CIRCLE FIVE, THE STYX, THE WRATHFUL;
CIRCLE SIX, DIS, CAPITAL OF HELL, THE FALLEN ANGELS. 1959–60
Solvent transfer drawing, pencil, watercolor, gouache, and crayon on paper, 14 1/2 x 11 1/2 in. (36.8 x 29.2 cm)
The Museum of Modern Art, New York. Given anonymously

Canto IX. *The Orchard (Circle Six)*

Wounded, the dead wait
        & do not heal—
instead, that's we the living

relearning to walk
        & to wake—
the smudge of lips

or blood. Breath.
        We're helpless, cannot
help but help

ourselves—& hope.
        The lizard who knows
loss means escape

        grows his tail back
within a week.

My father-
        in-law who lost
his spleen at twenty

has since grown back
        not one, but many.

The dog, three-headed, docked,
        chases where once
his tail wagged

        & was—each of us
this orchard of scars.

K.Y.

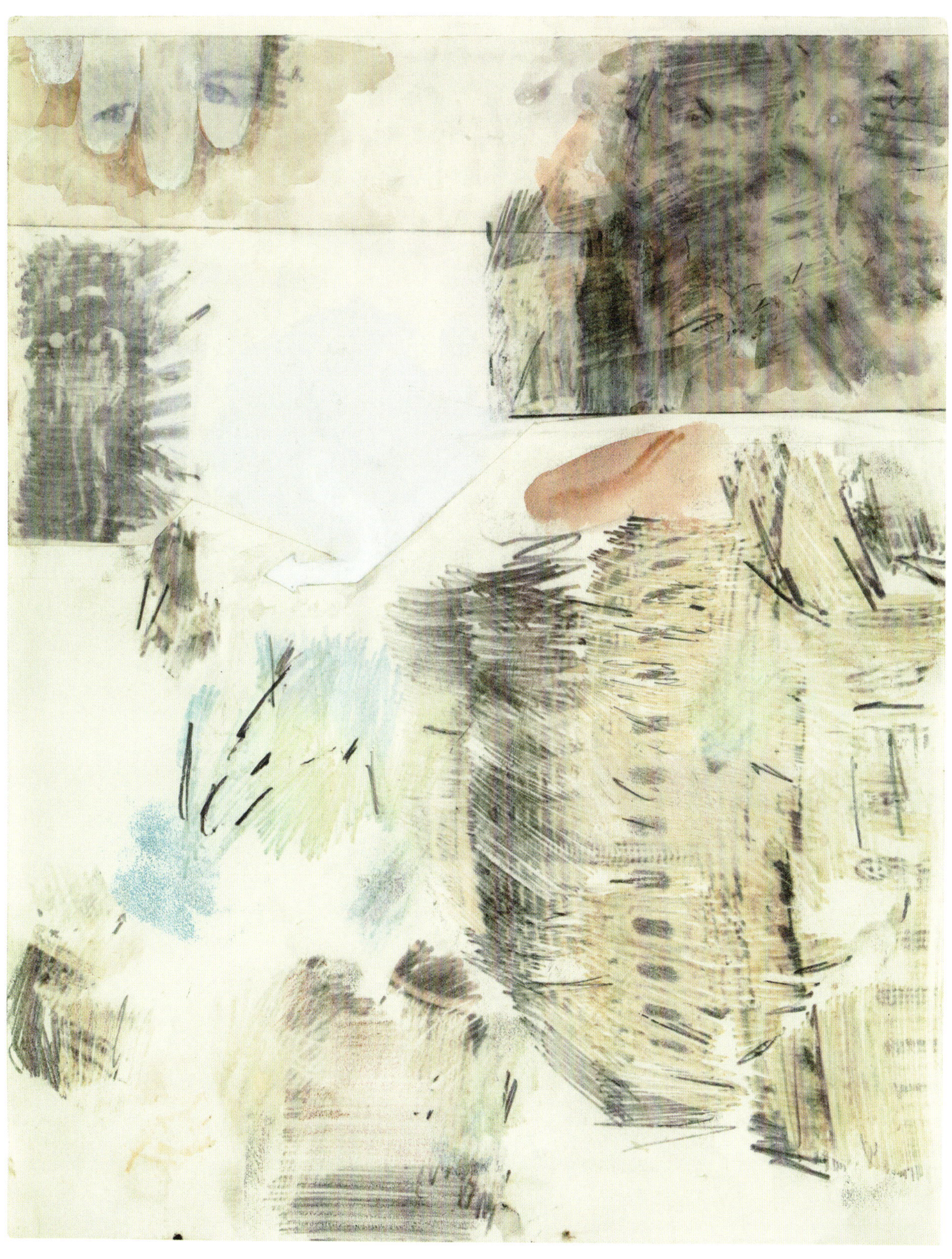

CANTO IX: CIRCLE SIX, THE HERETICS. 1959–60
Solvent transfer drawing, cut-and-pasted paper, watercolor, gouache, and crayon on paper, 14 1/2 x 11 1/2 in. (36.8 x 29.2 cm)
The Museum of Modern Art, New York. Given anonymously

Canto X. from *Necropolis*

Is there faith
        without belief?
Yes, it's known

as life in these parts.
        A steep stair.
Where we hail from

the storm sends its hail
        all a sudden, out
of nowhere & it rains

like nobody's business
        which is shuttered
with our windows.

Everything must go—
        even the stuffed swallows
& the sad, sewn giraffes

in the museum where nature
        believes history—
the hyenas made

of fur & wire
        who watch & grin
at whatever's missing.

K.Y.

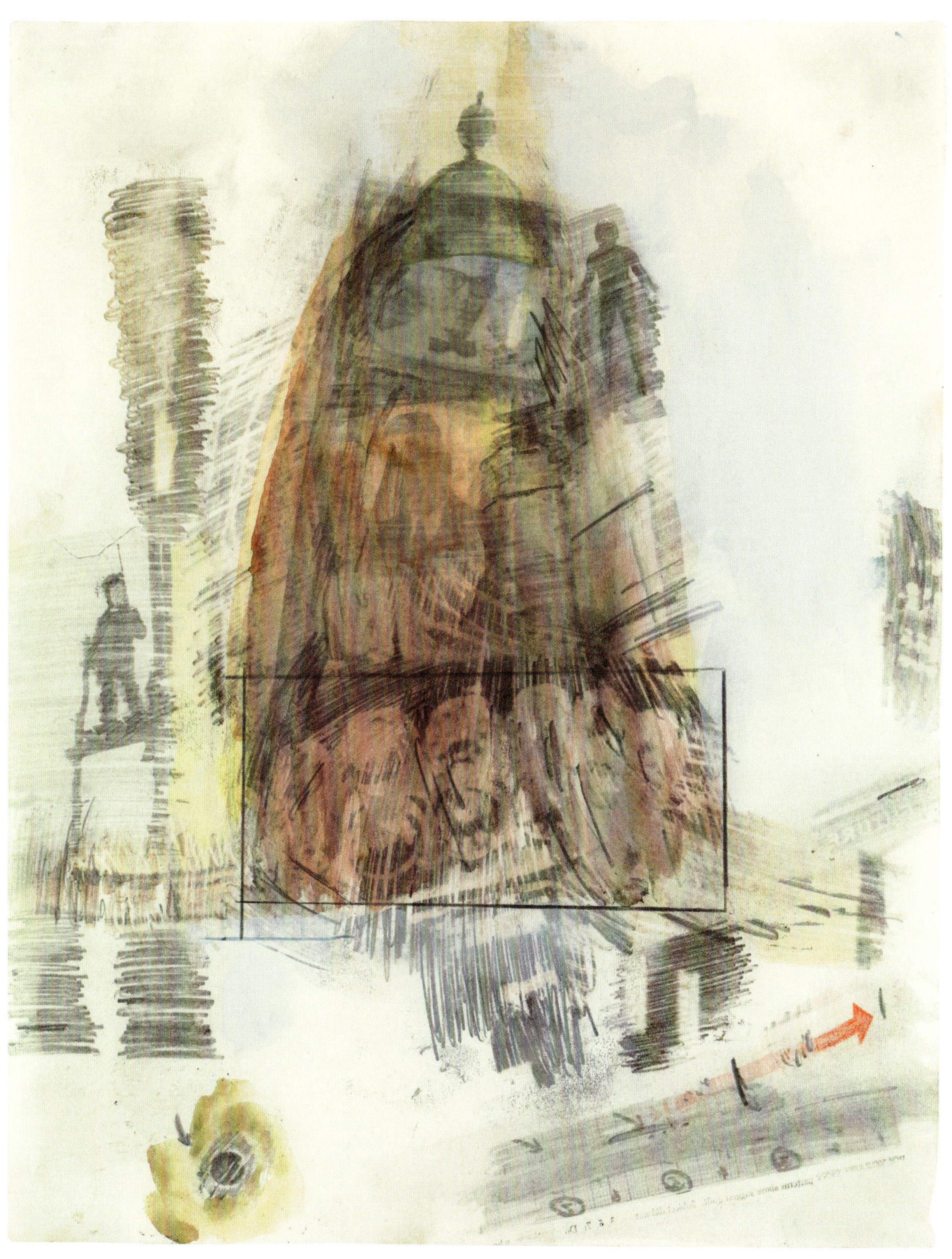

CANTO X: CIRCLE SIX, THE HERETICS. 1959–60
Solvent transfer drawing, watercolor, pencil, gouache, and crayon on paper, 14 1/2 x 11 3/8 in. (36.8 x 28.9 cm)
The Museum of Modern Art, New York. Given anonymously

Canto XI. *City of Dis (Circle Six: The Heretics)*

The dead won't leave
        us be. See
them crowd

the photograph at the edges,
        the negative,
unblinking in the glare

of the flash—
        their moment is over
& thus forever—

a still, a fraction
        of the will. What
keeps them never letting

us alone—companion,
        onion skin,
dark dog whose eyes

        the camera sees behind,
blooms white.

K.Y.

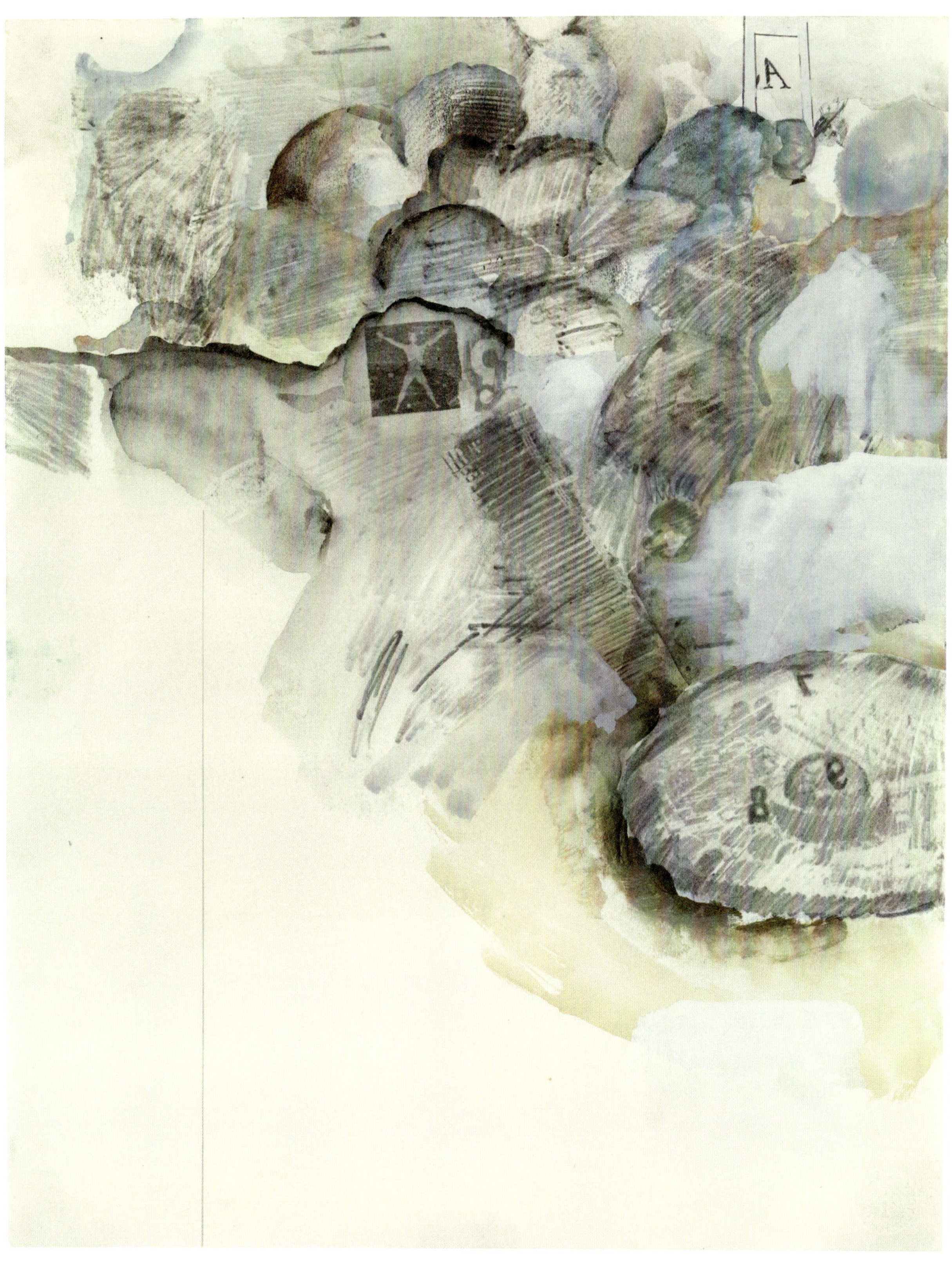

CANTO XI: CIRCLE SIX, THE HERETICS. 1959–60
Solvent transfer drawing, gouache, and pencil on paper, 14½ x 11⅜ in. (36.8 x 28.9 cm)
The Museum of Modern Art, New York. Given anonymously

Canto XII. *The Depths (Circle Seven, Round 1)*

The dead, newborn,
        need learn
a new tongue—

must learn to live
        with a body & not
inside one—

the innards' symphony.
        River of blood.
Enough, the infants cry.

Too much,
        say the dead,
who prefer to live

without pain
        or its opposite—
grace—the dead

all share the same
        fate—memory—
the figurehead of a ship,

salt-worn, grimaced, arms
        akimbo, fording
the faceless sea.

K.Y.

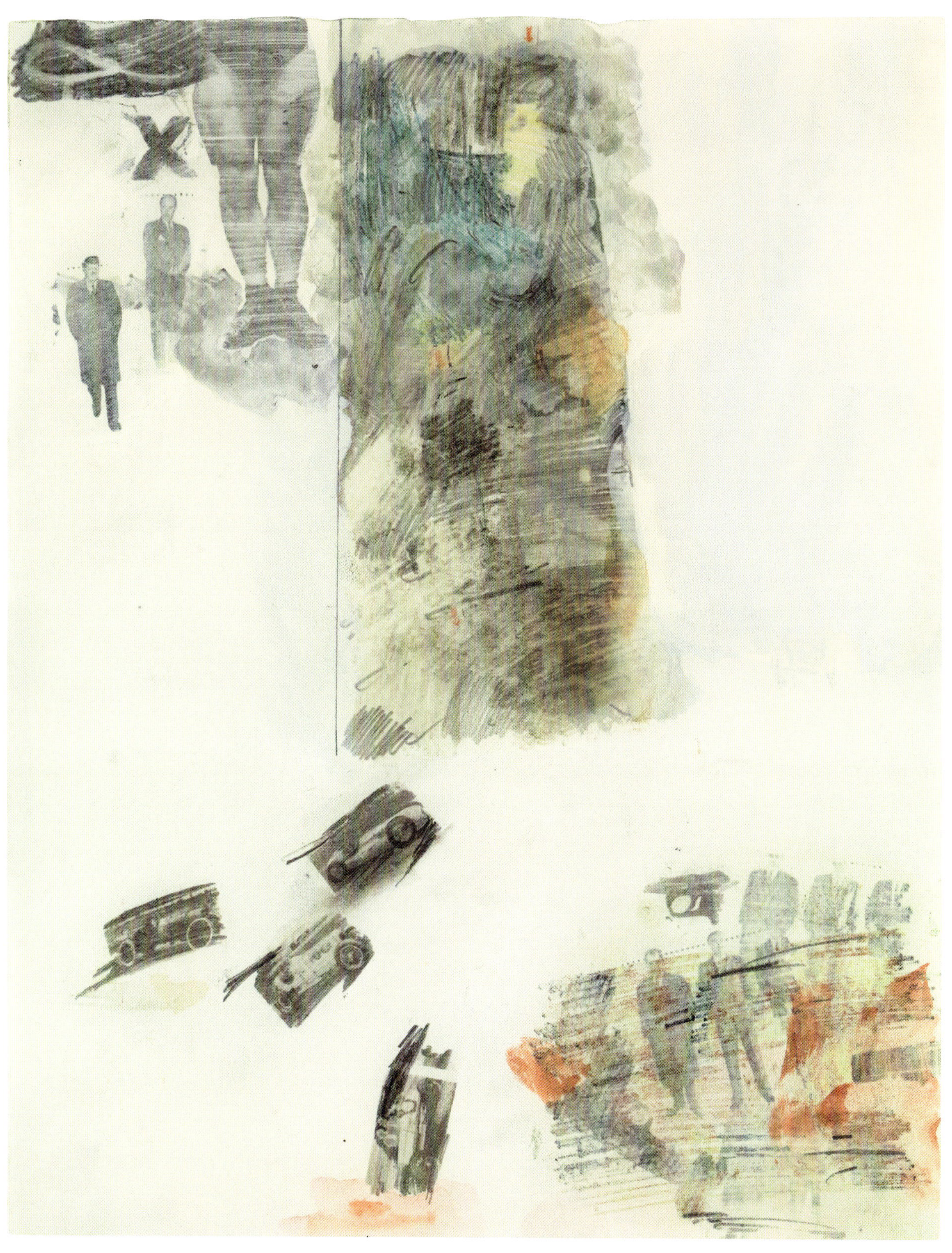

CANTO XII: CIRCLE SEVEN, ROUND 1, THE VIOLENT AGAINST NEIGHBORS. 1959–60
Solvent transfer drawing, watercolor, colored pencil, pencil, gouache, and black chalk on paper, 14 1/2 x 11 1/2 in. (36.8 x 29.2 cm)
The Museum of Modern Art, New York. Given anonymously

Canto XIII. *The Grove of Suicides (Circle Seven, Round 2)*

Why do they do
        themselves in,
why? Yet all I

can think to ask
        is how. Enormous
thorn. Bleeding leaf.

Silence
        other end of the line.
O wounded soul,

speak.

K.Y.

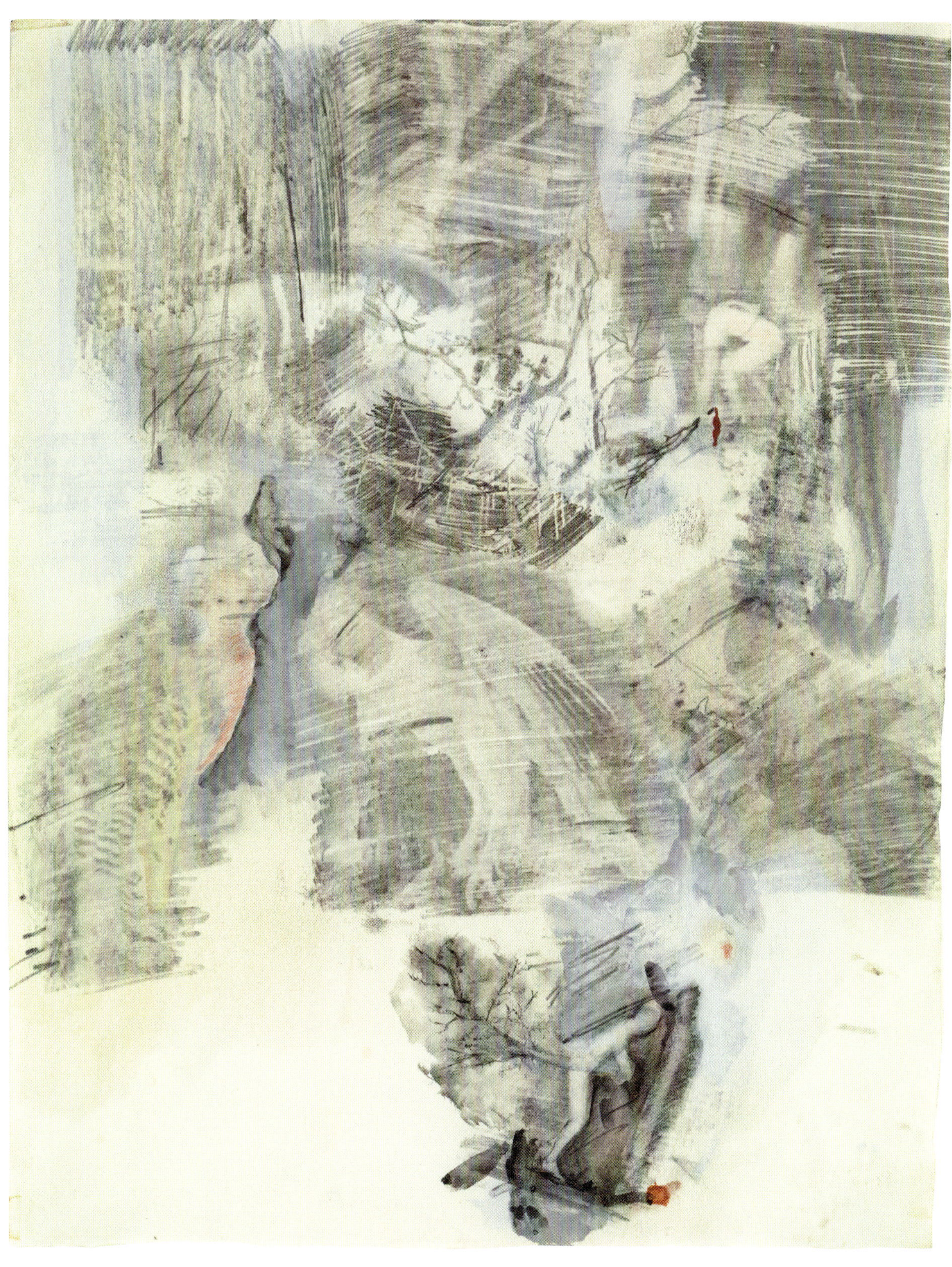

CANTO XIII: CIRCLE SEVEN, ROUND 2, THE VIOLENT AGAINST THEMSELVES. 1959–60
Solvent transfer drawing, gouache, pencil, colored pencil, watercolor, and
black chalk on paper, 14 1/2 x 11 3/8 in. (36.8 x 28.9 cm)
The Museum of Modern Art, New York. Given anonymously

Canto XIV. *Beyond (Circle Seven, Round 3)*

What if the body
        is what
we bring

with us
        beyond?
It is the soul

stays here, sullen,
        inconsolable,
not so much

wandering as waiting
        to be found
reunited, dirtied,

in the end—
        it is enough,
then, to see

the soul let loose only
        in those moments
of ecstasy, not when

we leave
        our body, but
when our body

arrives finally & our soul
        sups, fed
like the dead—

hands hungry
        as stray gloves.
Fingers may fill them

but still they need
        the noun
of the soul—

the soul's smell,
        its plangent
personhood. The more

they eat
        the more they need.
The body

always becoming—
        who verbs its way
over & under

while the soul rocks
        in the old folks'
home—the soul who

        shivers, grown
suddenly cold.

K.Y.

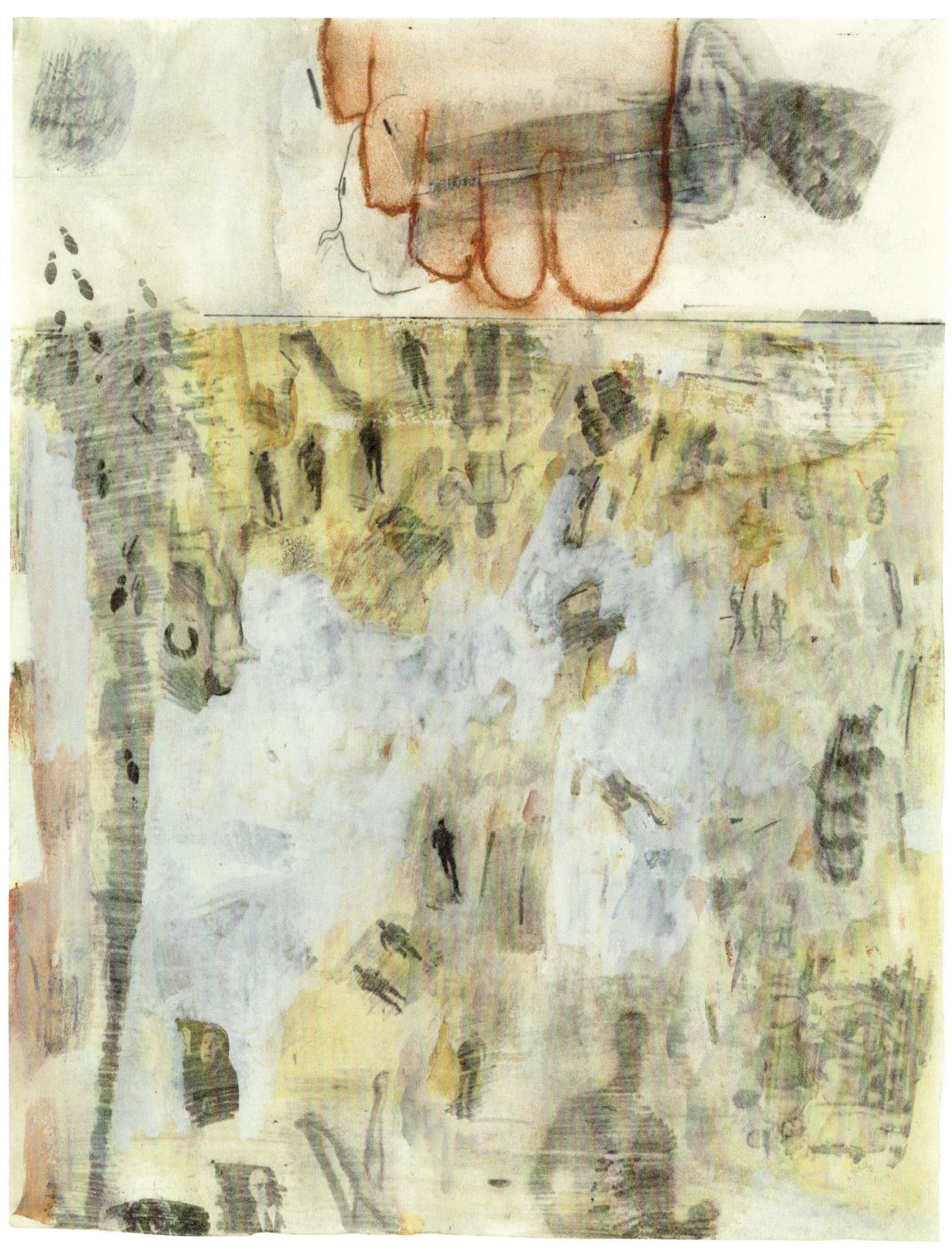

CANTO XIV: CIRCLE SEVEN, ROUND 3, THE VIOLENT AGAINST GOD, NATURE, AND ART. 1959–60
Solvent transfer drawing, watercolor, gouache, pencil, and
red chalk on paper, 14 3/8 x 11 1/2 in. (36.5 x 29.2 cm)
The Museum of Modern Art, New York. Given anonymously

Canto XV. *The Violent against Nature*

This stone margin: Now.

This shade flaming.

Constant threat of deluge.

The shores drown in spring's torrent.

The plan not so wide nor high.

Who designed this crossing so far from the woods?

The Dark Road pointing us toward the needle's eye.

Both sides hunger but never reach the grass.

We were all clerks of the one same crime—

Defiled Earth.

If you have any longing, run!
R.C.L.

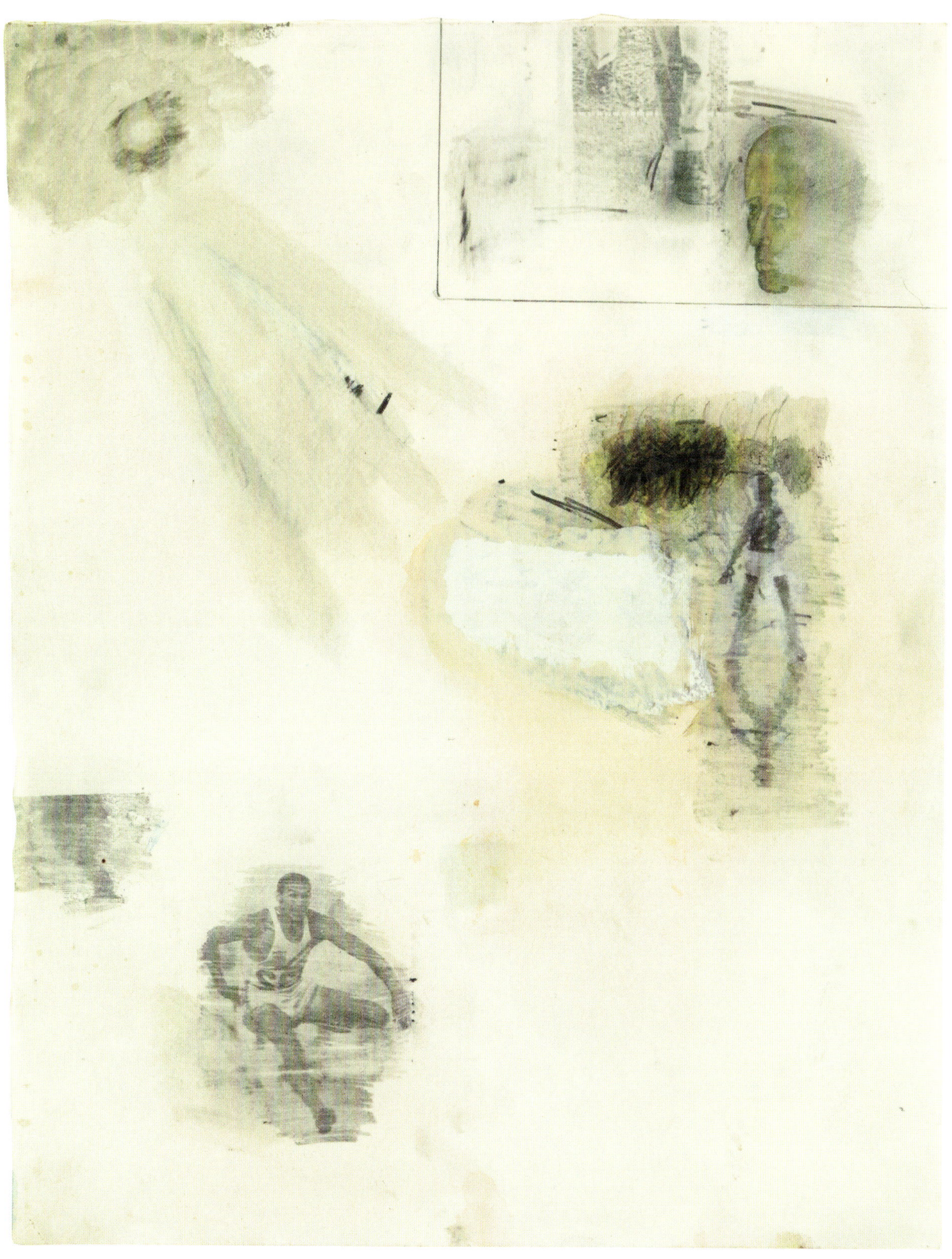

CANTO XV: CIRCLE SEVEN, ROUND 3, THE VIOLENT AGAINST NATURE. 1959–60
Solvent transfer drawing, gouache, watercolor, and
pencil on paper, 14 1/2 x 11 1/2 in. (36.8 x 29.2 cm)
The Museum of Modern Art, New York. Given anonymously

Canto XVI. *The Violent against Nature and Art*

Hear the rumbling
breaking toward us
from a company
that wants to
torture the rain—

the ancient wall
turning backward
to the misery of this place?
War: the first impulse of grief—

choked speech. This pit
men approach
with rehearsed *honor*,
led by the gall
of glory overweened.
The Heaven of Stars
speak of breaking,

their *Amen*,
pronounced bound,
habit all coiled and wound.
Out from the edge
. . . a long bottomless
darkness.

Intent's arms
spread upward,
feet drawn
close.

R.C.L.

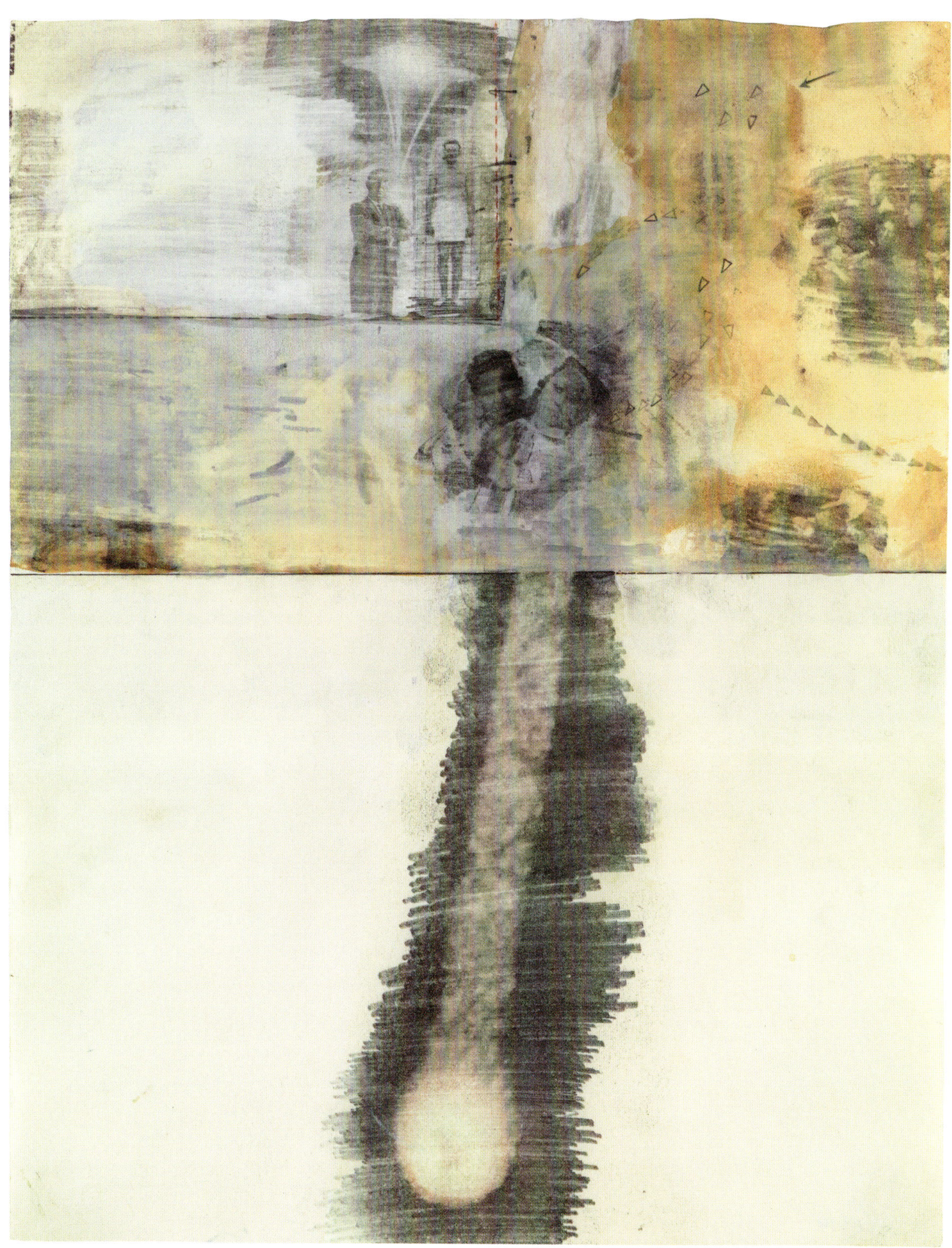

CANTO XVI: CIRCLE SEVEN, ROUND 3, THE VIOLENT AGAINST NATURE AND ART. 1959–60
Solvent transfer drawing, watercolor, pencil, colored pencil, and
gouache on paper, 14 3/8 x 11 3/8 in. (36.5 x 28.9 cm)
The Museum of Modern Art, New York. Given anonymously

Canto XVII.

"Now see the sharp-tailed beast
that mounts the brink..."

These words signal the sheer end
of our rocky prototype.

Fraud settles his head upon the edge
of a dark innocence under his body.

Features and expressions half-reptile—
Paws, knots, circlets:

Tapestry of flowering
Void.

A fight is on—
The rim bound, burning—

Monster—crouching
on the ledge,

smoking hands, blood
whiter than sorrow,

purse twisted, tongue licking
its rump, undaunted,

(backward, backward)
the sky a great scar—

leaned out and stared
into Hell.

R.C.L.

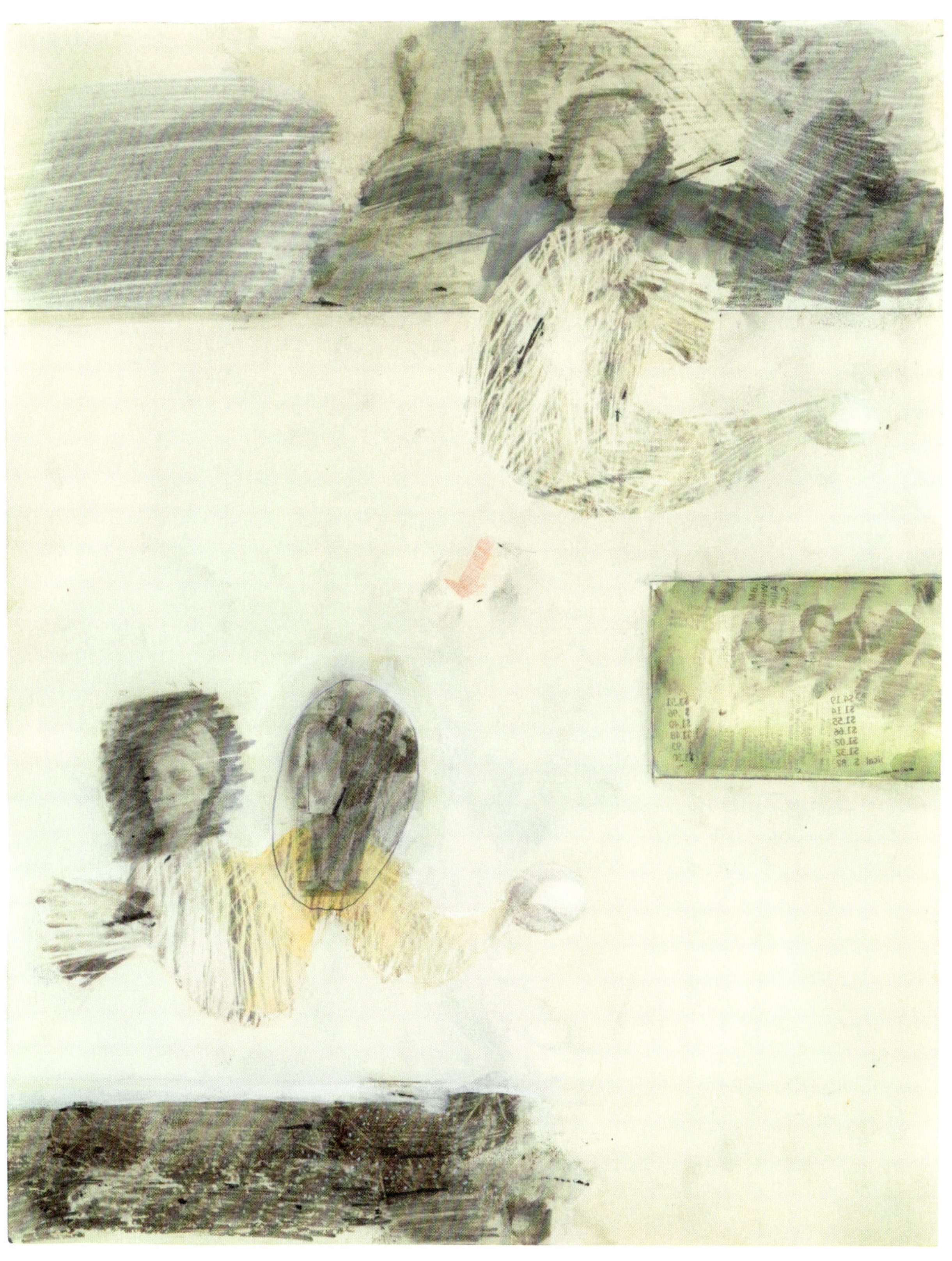

CANTO XVII: CIRCLE SEVEN, ROUND 3,
THE VIOLENT AGAINST ART, THE USURERS, GERYON. 1959–60
Solvent transfer drawing, gouache, and pencil on paper, 14 1/2 x 11 1/2 in. (36.8 x 29.2 cm)
The Museum of Modern Art, New York. Given anonymously

Canto XVIII.

"You there, Who Walk Alone
with Your Eyes on The Ground…"

Is Hell a vast and sloping ground,
a lost place that yawns
wide and deep—

or a proper orange border
that remains between
the *well* and the *great*?

Enormous wall girded many times 'round.
On one side: "Toward!"
On the other: "Move along!"

Quick march, first crack
of the face: a procession.
Kindness took a few steps back.

You that walk alone
with your eyes on the ground,
I know you, unwillingly.

In your living voice
I hear the World stir
that sordid old tale, tales

of avarice, of lashes fell.
Move on, Pimp, there are
no women here to sell.

Turn away, turn the jagged crest—
What kingliness Hell is made of,
honeyed tongue and dishonest.

Forsakened people in a river
of excrement. I knew you when
your hair was dry, Clown-Head.

Flatteries sold among the dead. Lean forward
a bit, look. See that one scratching
her crouch past all believing?

R.C.L.

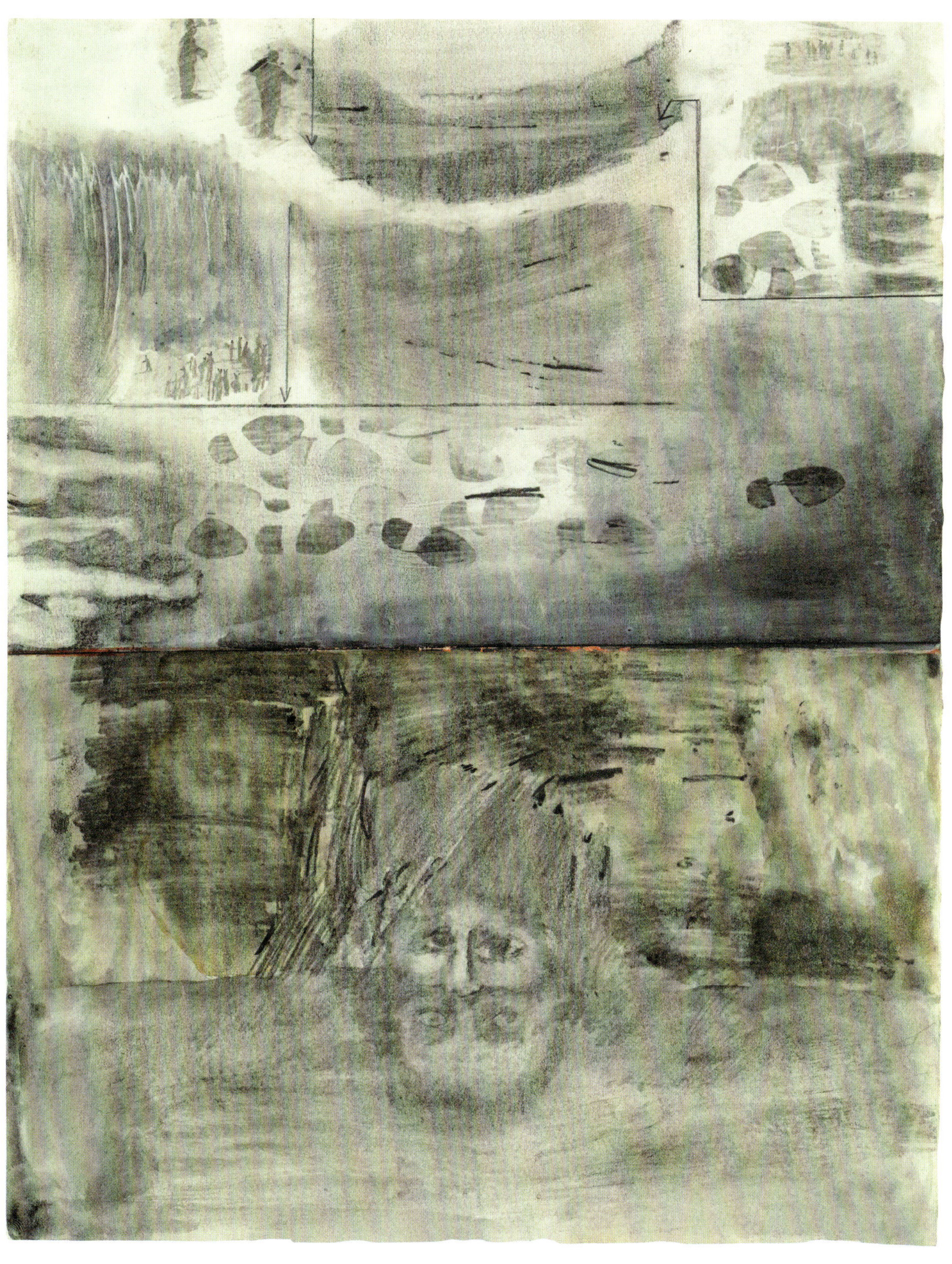

CANTO XVIII: CIRCLE EIGHT, MALEBOLGE, THE EVIL DITCHES, THE FRAUDULENT AND MALICIOUS: BOLGIA 1, THE PANDERERS AND SEDUCERS; BOLGIA 2, THE FLATTERERS. 1959–60
Solvent transfer drawing, pencil, gouache, and crayon on paper, 14 1/2 x 11 1/2 in. (36.8 x 29.2 cm)
The Museum of Modern Art, New York. Given anonymously

Canto XIX.

"O wretched crew, who follow HIM,
pandering for silver and gold the things
of God which should be wedded to love
and righteousness! Oh THIEVES
for hire, now must the TRUMP
of judgment sound your doom,
here in the third fosse of the rim
of fire…Soles all ABLAZE!"

We had already made our way
across the midpoint of wisdom,

Thine art doth shine in Heaven, on Earth,
how justly doth thy power judge and assign!

along the wall and on the ground
we broke open,

Whoever you are, sad spirit, who lie here
with your head below your heels planted
like a stake—speak if you can

every mouth a sinner
in the throes of leaping higher.

Are you already sated with treasure
for which you dared to turn on the Sweet Lady
and trick and pluck and bleed her at your pleasure?

Virtuous She Who Sits upon the Waters,
born with seven heads, ten enormous shining horns,

Selling holy office!

make her glad as love and virtue please
with both arms remount the rocky path, hold me.

Stay as you are. This hole well fits you—

Clasp the arch which crosses the pits of woe.
Arrive tenderly to that ledge, look down another moat.
R.C.L.

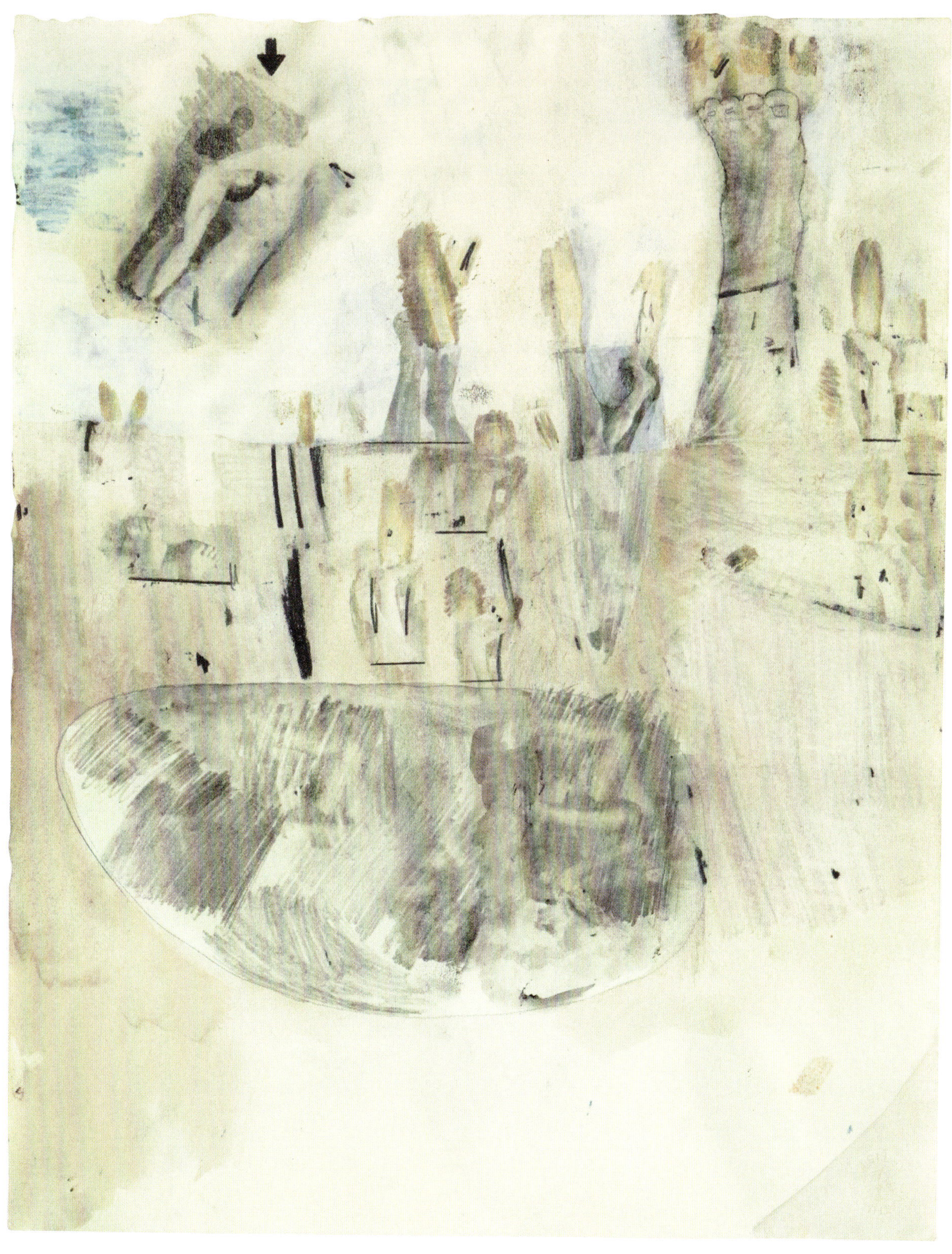

CANTO XIX: CIRCLE EIGHT, BOLGIA 3, THE SIMONIACS. 1959–60
Solvent transfer drawing, gouache, and pencil on paper, 14 3/8 x 11 1/2 in. (36.5 x 29.2 cm)
The Museum of Modern Art, New York. Given anonymously

Canto XX.

Canto of pain, clear view
of desolation, procession of faces
reversed on the neck, staring
backwards: *before* forbidden.
R.C.L.

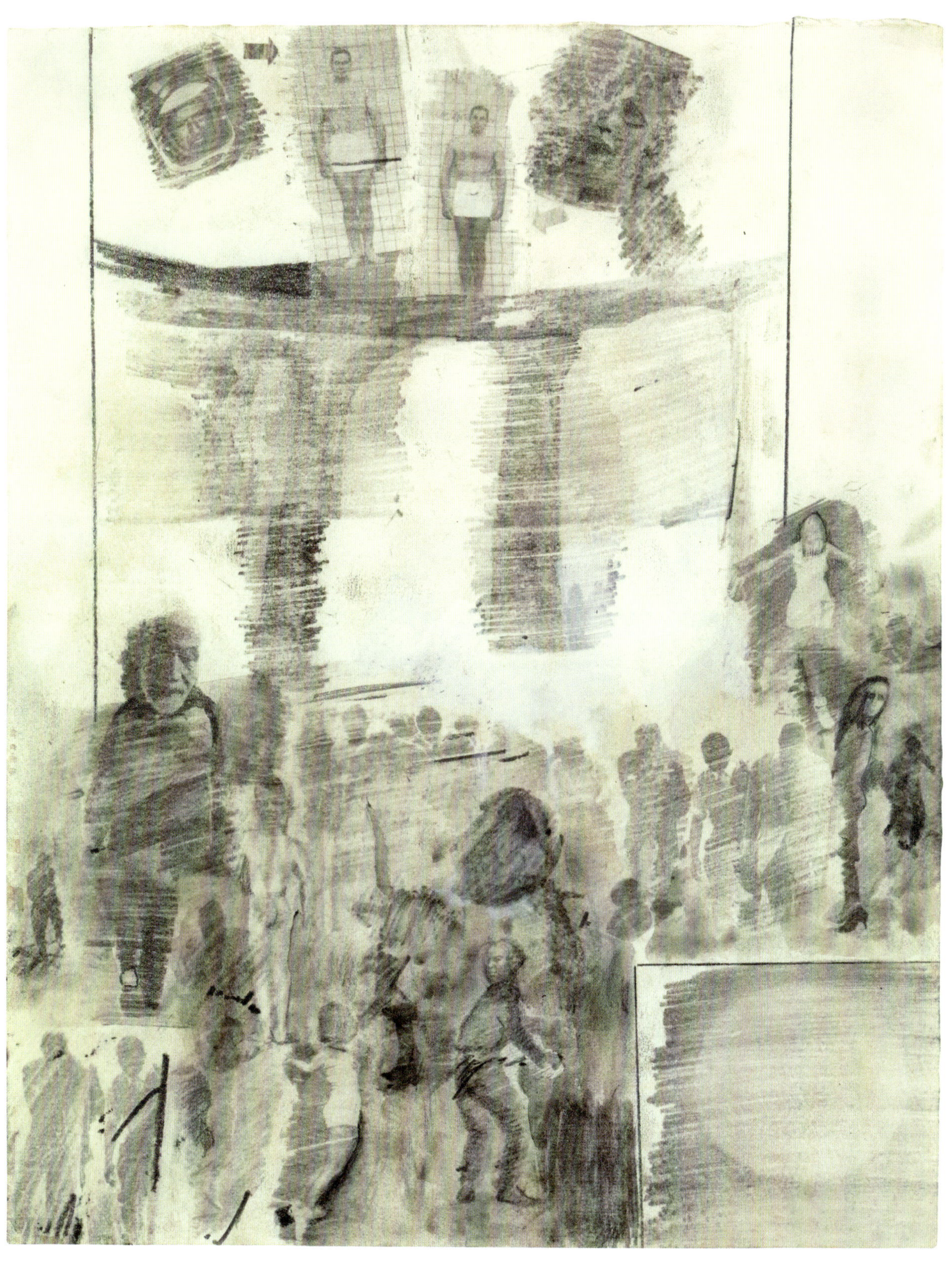

CANTO XX: CIRCLE EIGHT, BOLGIA 4, THE FORTUNE TELLERS AND DIVINERS. 1959–60
Solvent transfer drawing and pencil on paper, 14 1/2 x 11 1/2 in. (36.8 x 29.2 cm)
The Museum of Modern Art, New York. Given anonymously

Canto XXI.

Competing with Terror,
Hate and Wildness—Galloping—
Wings outspread—Bitter—
Each high-hunched shoulder—A Sinner.

Here the Sacred Face looks
With more than a hundred hooks.
No one checks your books, Scullery Boy,
you had best not be seen. *This dread state.*

Whatever violence you cause through this
walk on the bridge, all the House
(Shall I give him a touch in the rump?
Sure: give him a taste to pay him for his bother!)

At ease, there, Snatcher!
There's no road on this side.
All-in-Pieces-Boy, gentleman-molested
in the name of Heaven.

Go on alone (Who can trust
such an escort?). Pointed-Tongue Captain,
wishing permission to pass, after
they made a trumpet of his ass.

R.C.L.

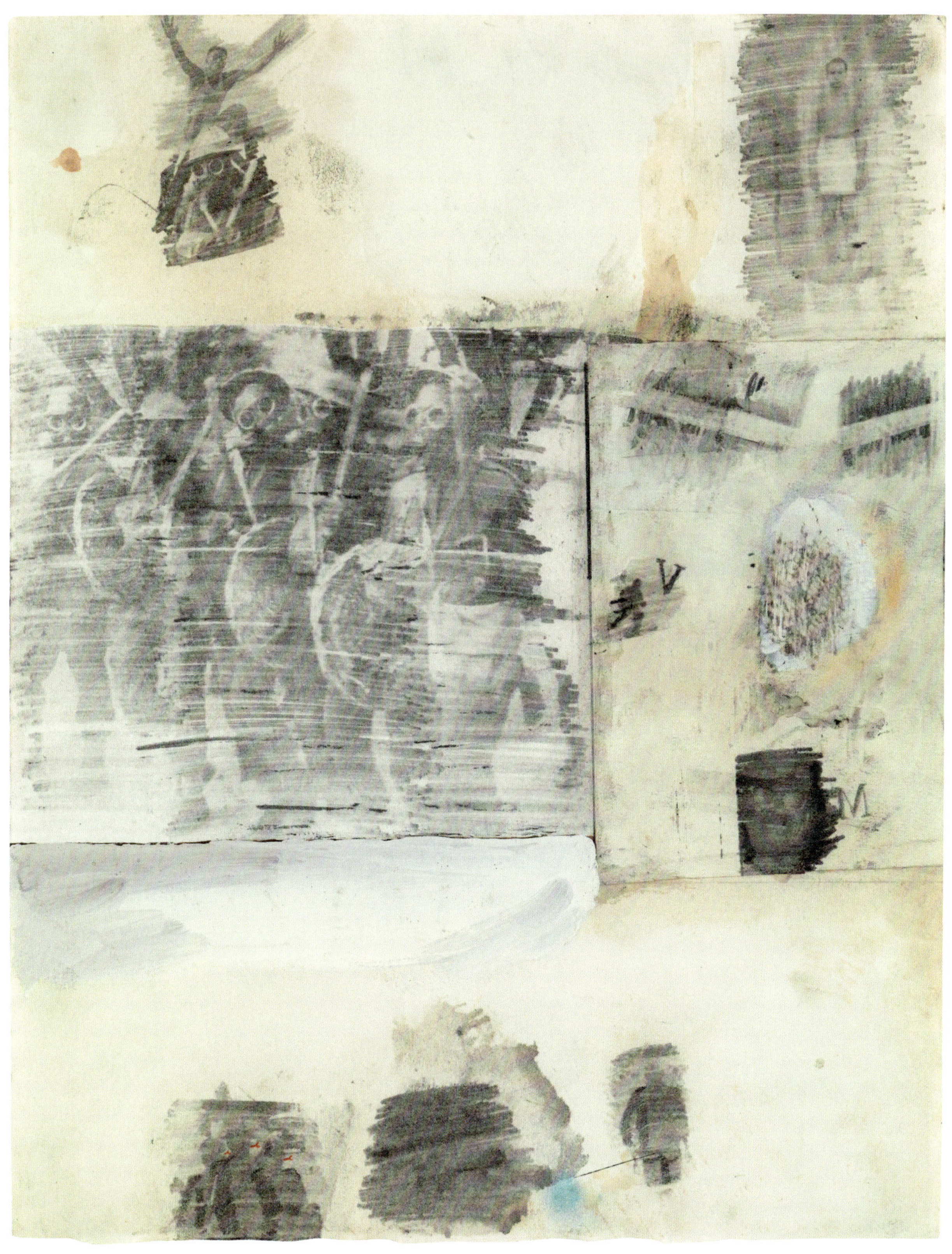

CANTO XXI: CIRCLE EIGHT, BOLGIA 5, THE GRAFTERS. 1959–60
Solvent transfer drawing, gouache, cut-and-pasted paper, pencil, and colored pencil on paper, 14 3/8 x 11 1/2 in. (36.5 x 29.2 cm)
The Museum of Modern Art, New York. Given anonymously

Canto XXII.

"But never have I seen in horse or foot,
nor ship in range of land nor sight of star,
take its direction from so low a toot."

The beginning of assault.
March and muster. Trampled land.
Columns of shock. Endless lines

Fall-to and begin
to secure ship
above the pitch.

(There is much more
that I should like to tell you, but oh,
I think he means to grate my hide!)
R.C.L.

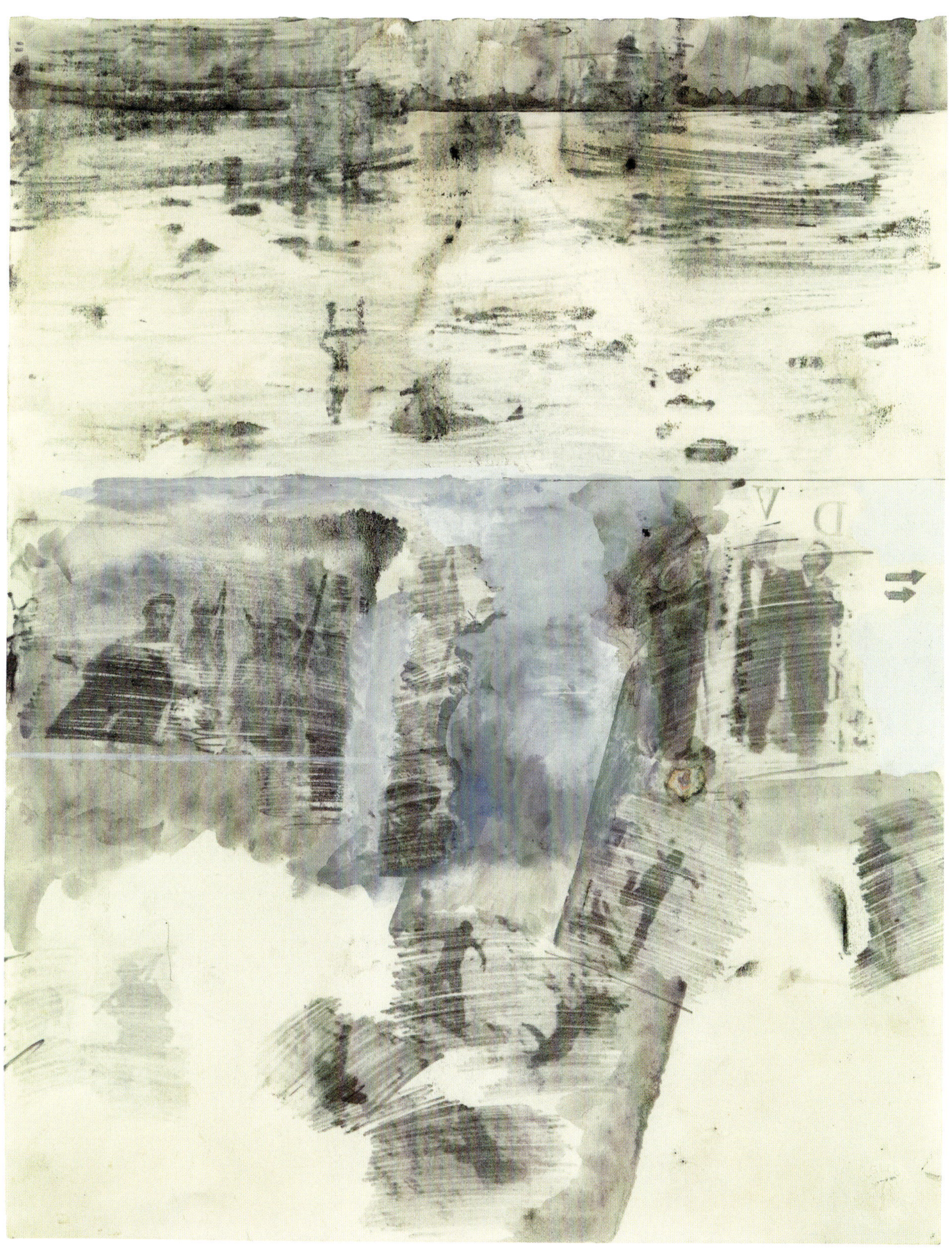

CANTO XXII: CIRCLE EIGHT, BOLGIA 5, THE GRAFTERS. 1959–60
Solvent transfer drawing, gouache, and pencil on paper, 14 3/8 x 11 1/2 in. (36.5 x 29.2 cm)
The Museum of Modern Art, New York. Given anonymously

Canto XXIII.

"I Go with The Body That Was Always Mine"

Silent, one following the other,
the Fable hunted us down.
O weary mantle of eternity,
turn left, reach us down
into that narrow way in silence.

College of Sorry Hypocrites, I go
with the body that was always mine,
burnished like counterweights to keep
the peace. One may still see the sort of peace

we kept. Marvel for a while over that:
the cross in Hell's eternal exile.
Somewhere there is some gap in the wall,
pit through which we may climb

to the next brink without the need
of summoning the Black Angels
and forcing them to raise us from this sink.
Nearer than *hope*, there is a bridge

that runs from the great circle, that crosses
every ditch from ridge to ridge.
Except—it is broken—but with care.

R.C.L.

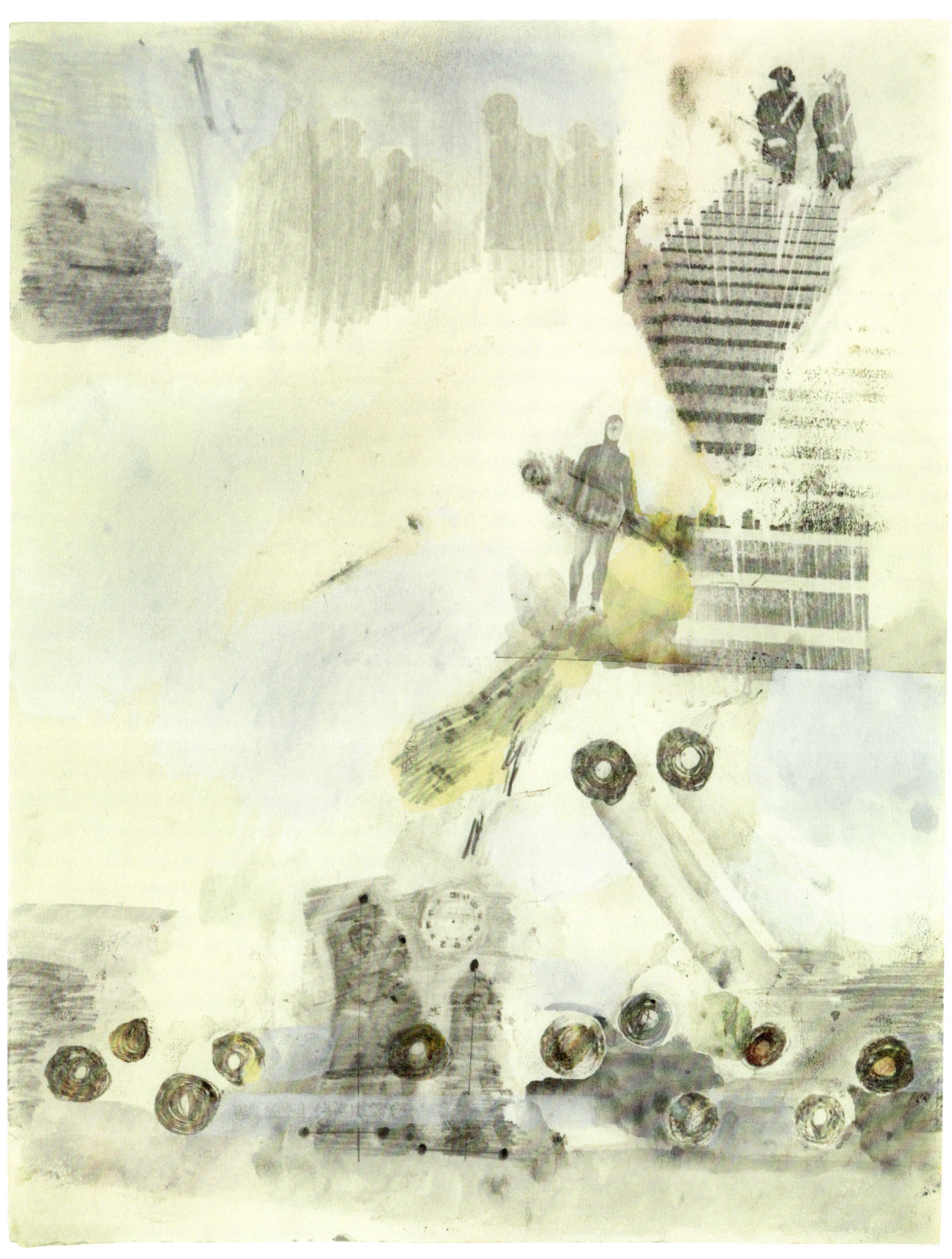

CANTO XXIII: CIRCLE EIGHT, BOLGIA 6, THE HYPOCRITES. 1959–60
Solvent transfer drawing, pencil, gouache, and
watercolor on paper, 14 3/8 x 11 1/2 in. (36.5 x 29.2 cm)
The Museum of Modern Art, New York. Given anonymously

Canto XXIV. *Whore-Frost, Fifty-Six Percent*

Who Needs Niggers?
Down with Martin Luther Coon
Jews! Jews! Jews Everywhere!

—text detail from Robert Rauschenberg's
Drawings for Dante's 700th Birthday

The image of his white sister on the ground—

The first son wipes away the work of the peasants—

See the fields? All-white lambs beat then smite their thighs—

Go back into the house, come out again, Despair

How the Earth's face changed in so little time

Take the staffs their lambs—feed their plasters, their sores—

Lead-Hung Hypocrites hand-hold by holding hands—

There is a longer ladder (yet) to climb...

...steeper, more jagged than any we've crossed up to this time

I know what is said: No other answer than the *act*—

Great coils of memory hide, hands bound, knotted, behind torment—

Mule-among-Men, Man-of-Blood-and-Anger who stole the treasure from the Sacristy

Emptied of the Black Party and Her Laws, the God of War brings back

A vapor wrapped in a storm; the vapor breaks apart

The mist, and there: *Every White shall feel his wounds anew*—

And have I told you this that it may grieve you?

R.C.L.

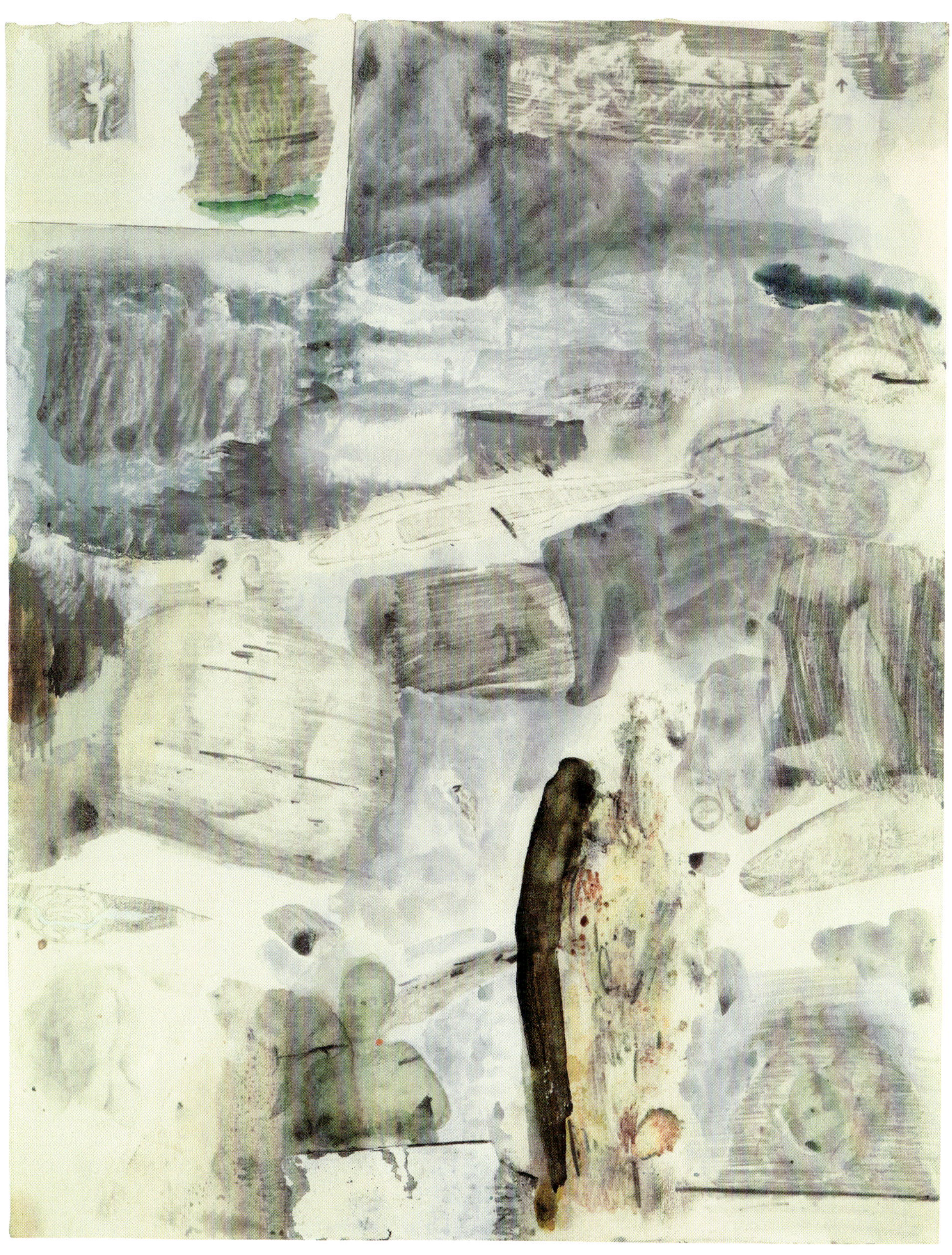

CANTO XXIV: CIRCLE EIGHT, BOLGIA 7, THE THIEVES. 1959–60
Solvent transfer drawing, gouache, watercolor, and
pencil on paper, 14 3/8 x 11 1/2 in. (36.5 x 29.2 cm)
The Museum of Modern Art, New York. Given anonymously

Canto XXV.

"In all of Hell's corrupt and sunken halls
I found no shade so arrogant toward God"

The snake became my friend.
Lake of blood, my talk fell still.

I saw my own eyes color
together until neither appeared. The edge

of heat, the burning page, discoloration
changes to black as white dies from the sheet.

Look on, alas! Neither two nor one,
blurred and blended, neither face began

or ended. Likenesses mottled to both
and neither: Be still, History!

(Wounded below the eyes, face
of the prostrate, forked tongue

that has become a beast,
talking and spitting.

Remain crawling along
this road as I have done

Shift,
reshift).

R.C.L.

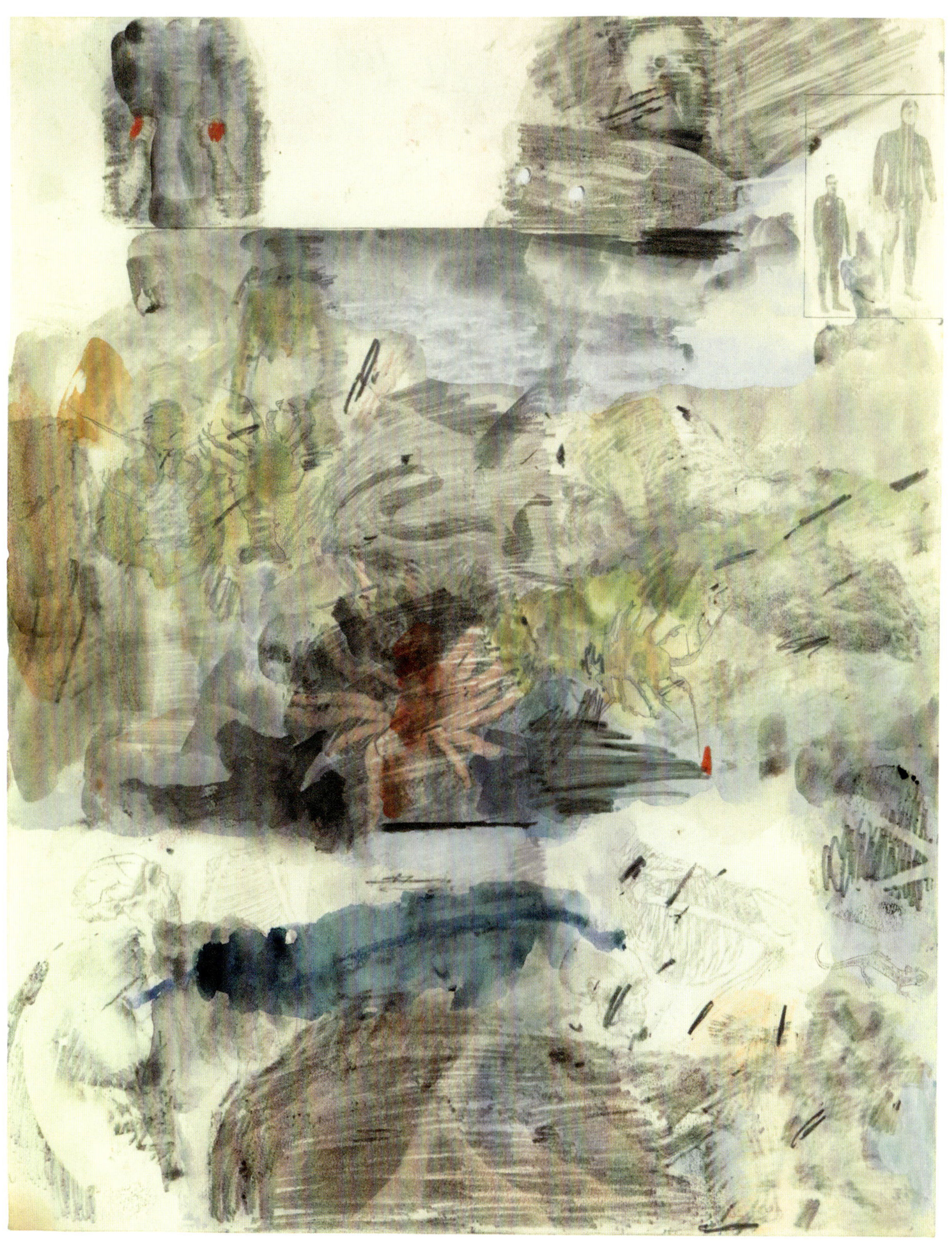

CANTO XXV: CIRCLE EIGHT, BOLGIA 7, THE THIEVES. 1959–60
Solvent transfer drawing, watercolor, colored pencil, and
pencil on paper, 14 3/8 x 11 1/2 in. (36.5 x 29.2 cm)
The Museum of Modern Art, New York. Given anonymously

Canto XXVI. *The Evil Counselors*

Citizens:

If the truth dreamed of this morning
shall mount honor, peopling,
You shall feel what others
wish for you. So may it come.

Truth dreams of morning, climbs,
stone by stone, the natural stair,
and going lonely through that dead
land again—stars merit fireflies—
The horses ride the flames.

High sea, stay true
when the rest desert me.
Warn all men back
from their voyage—
on the left, on the right.
Press on toward recognition.

Raise all the stars.
Seas close over us.

R.C.L.

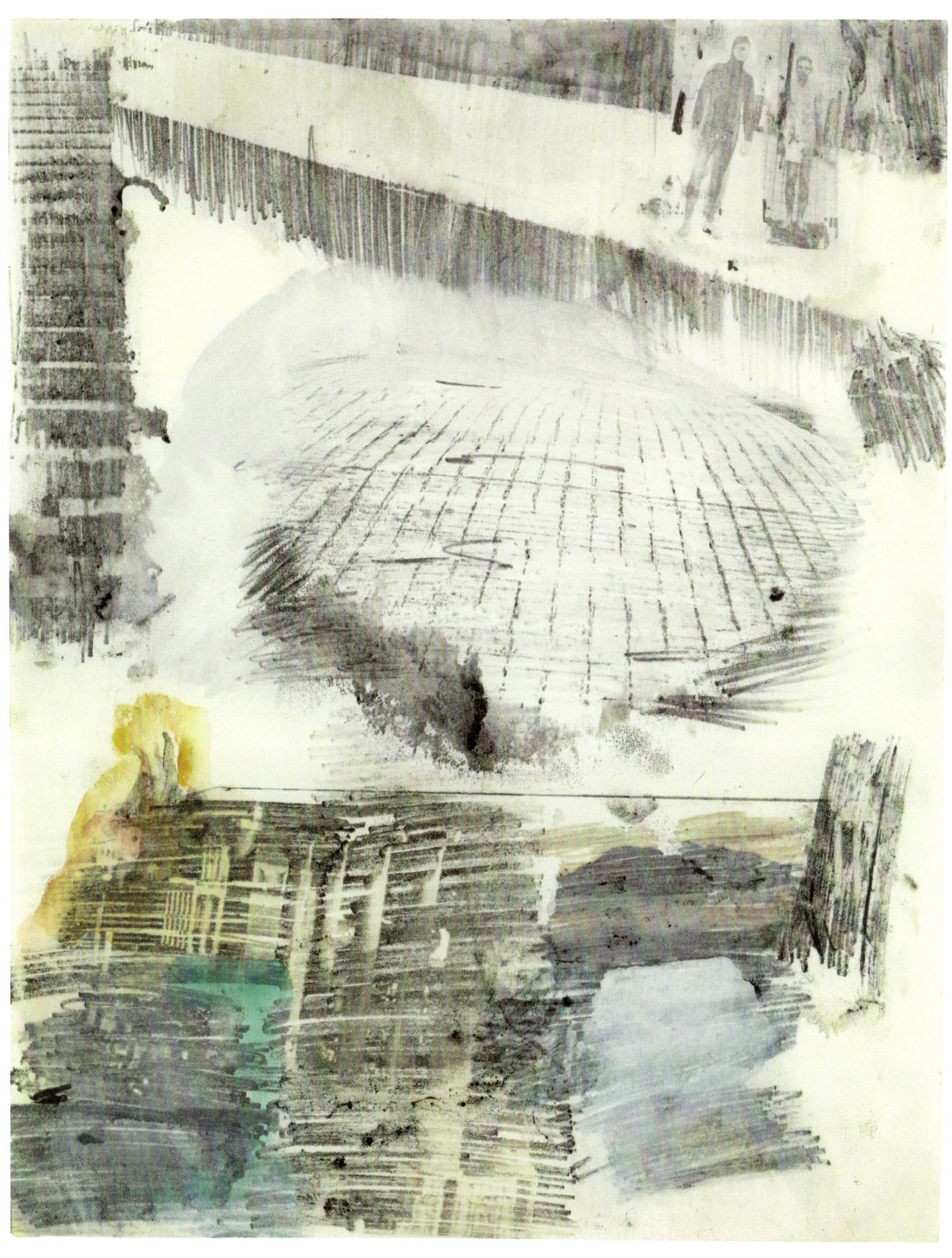

CANTO XXVI: CIRCLE EIGHT, BOLGIA 8, THE EVIL COUNSELORS. 1959–60
Solvent transfer drawing, watercolor, and
pencil on paper, 14 3/8 x 11 1/2 in. (36.5 x 29.2 cm)
The Museum of Modern Art, New York. Given anonymously

Canto XXVII. *The Evil Counselors*

Finish speaking, Great Flame!

Our attention turned
strange, muffled, burned—

Brazen?

Lament.

Mournful words were changed into
a found tongue of the concealed Spirit

Oh you at whom I aim my voice

—I may come a bit late to my turn,

May it not annoy you to pause
and speak a while. You see
it does not annoy me—and I burn

I have fallen only recently
to this blind world. Pray, tell me,
is there peace or war on earth?

The Lion changes his politics with a compass
Still encased in the pulp Mother bore from birth

Clean me here. Lift me, carry me
'round the coiled fire.

I am lost accordingly—

Grieving heart—

Attire

R.C.L.

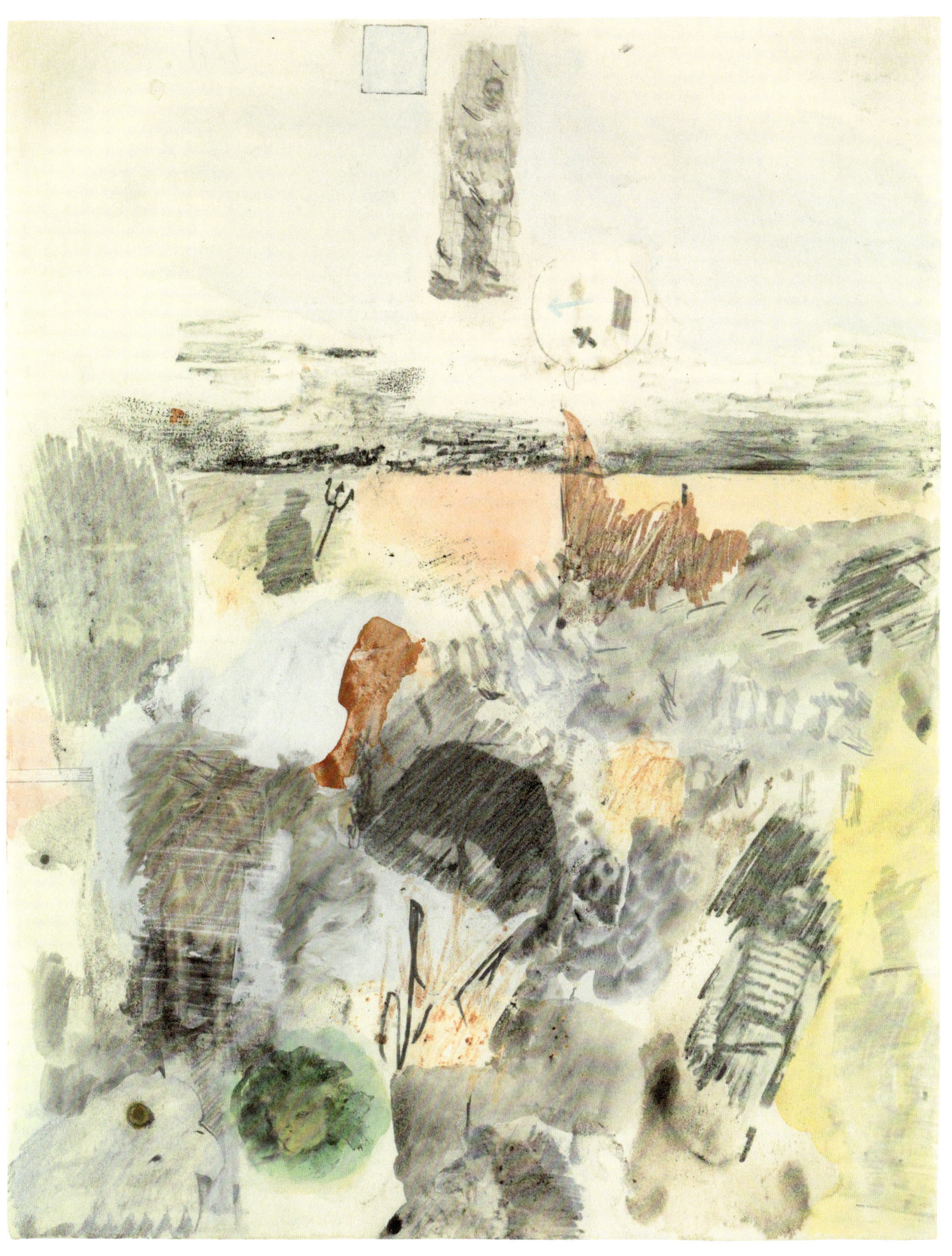

CANTO XXVII: CIRCLE EIGHT, BOLGIA 8, THE EVIL COUNSELORS. 1959–60
Solvent transfer drawing, watercolor, gouache, and
pencil on paper, 14 3/8 x 11 3/8 in. (36.5 x 28.9 cm)
The Museum of Modern Art, New York. Given anonymously

Canto XXVIII. *The Sowers of Discord*

"Who Could Describe in Words Set Free...
The Blood and Wounds that Now Were Shown to Me!"

Grief-deep languages,
vocabulary of pain,
fateful soil running
the blood-long war,

spoil of golden rings
won without weapons,
the Mutilation opened
wide. Red guts,

the heart, the lungs,
gallbladder, shriveled
sac shit mangled and split.
History cannot speak—

A wretch *with a bloody stump*
in his throat in place of a tongue.
R.C.L.

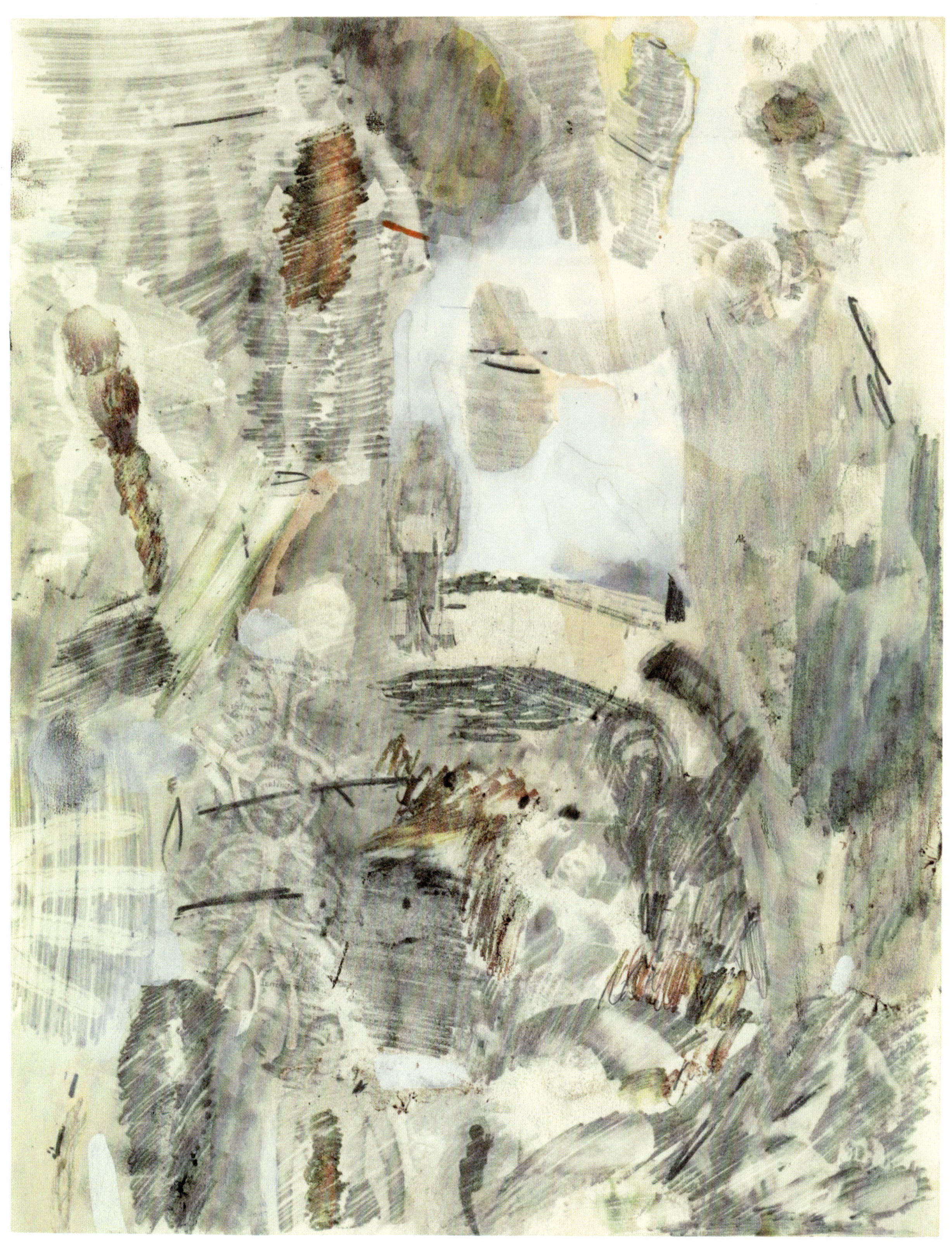

CANTO XXVIII: CIRCLE EIGHT, BOLGIA 9, THE SOWERS OF DISCORD:
THE SOWERS OF RELIGIOUS AND POLITICAL DISCORD BETWEEN KINSMEN. 1959–60
Solvent transfer drawing, pencil, watercolor, gouache, and colored pencil on paper, 14 1/2 x 11 1/2 in. (36.8 x 29.2 cm)
The Museum of Modern Art, New York. Given anonymously

Canto XXIX.

Parade of broken dead
stare from the shadows

under our feet—outspread
brethren in my hands.

Death sits like a presence
on marsh air. Still.

Every beast down
to the smallest worm

gasping and crawling
on hands and knees,

one against the other.
The furious burning itch

as they scrub and claw themselves.
Men in the first world live for many suns.

Tell me how to raise myself
and fly through the air.

R.C.L.

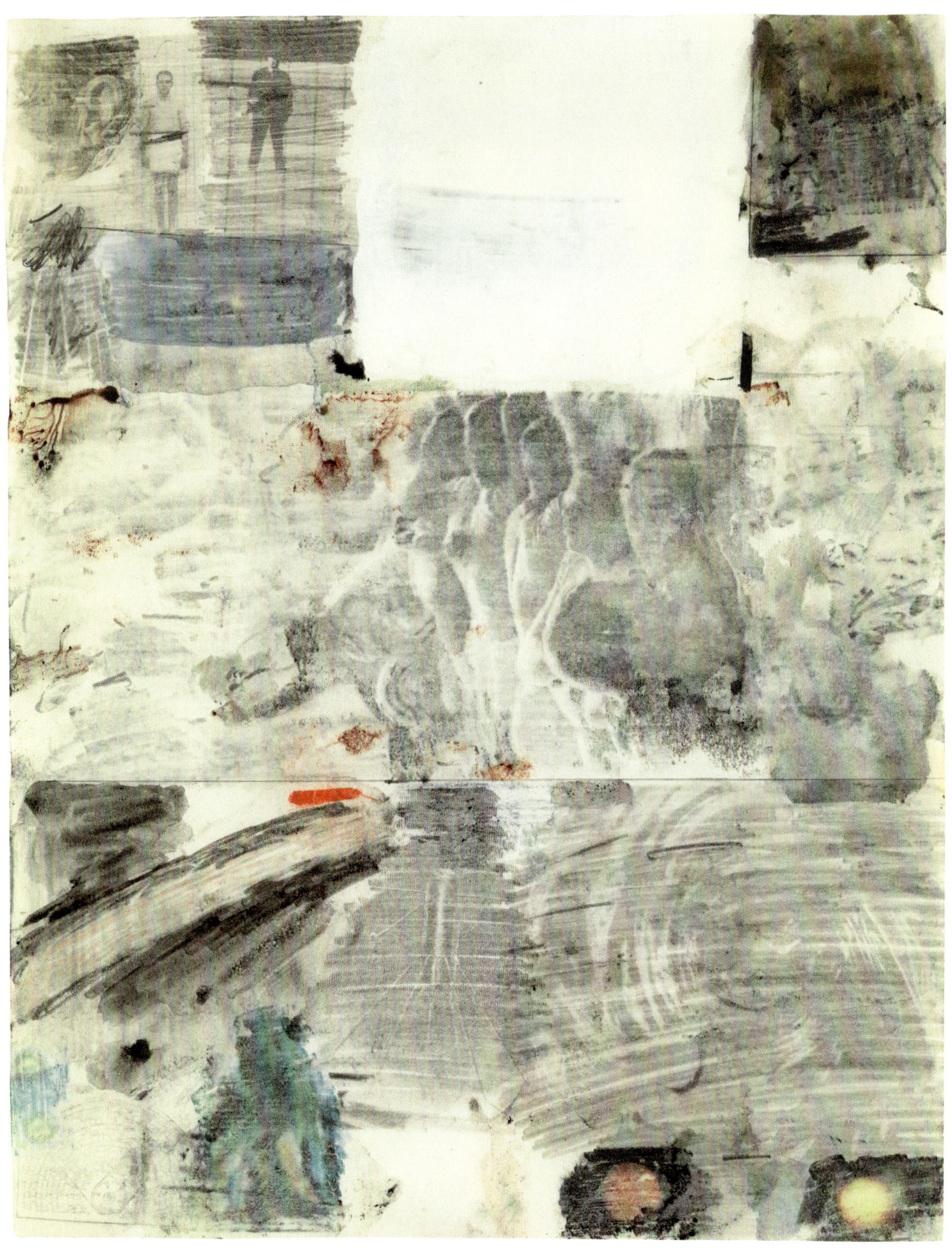

CANTO XXIX: CIRCLE EIGHT, BOLGIA 10, THE FALSIFIERS: CLASS 1, THE ALCHEMISTS. 1959–60
Solvent transfer drawing, pastel, gouache, watercolor, and
pencil on paper, 14 1/2 x 11 1/2 in. (36.8 x 29.2 cm)
The Museum of Modern Art, New York. Given anonymously

Canto XXX. *Self-Portrait as Rauschenberg's Biography*

The house, nets across the pass. The sea. Alone beside the alien sea. Naked and clean. Running towards us, hungry after night. Trembling. Life sank its teeth in you. Pleased to tell us what shade is before it raced on. Loved with more rightful love. Form came disguised with him. A testament to observe the misbegotten. Spirits that lay about. Another husk, a mandolin, limbs, lips thrust forward, a sick man, this grim world.

(In my first lifetime I had enough to please me here)

Imagination dries me more than disease. The inflexible image bound and burned—an inch in a hundred years. I started off from freaks. Because of them I like here persuaded. Smokes in winter when it first rains. Presentation rigid when noting will answer. Your last walk, free as it was when you were coming.

R.C.L.

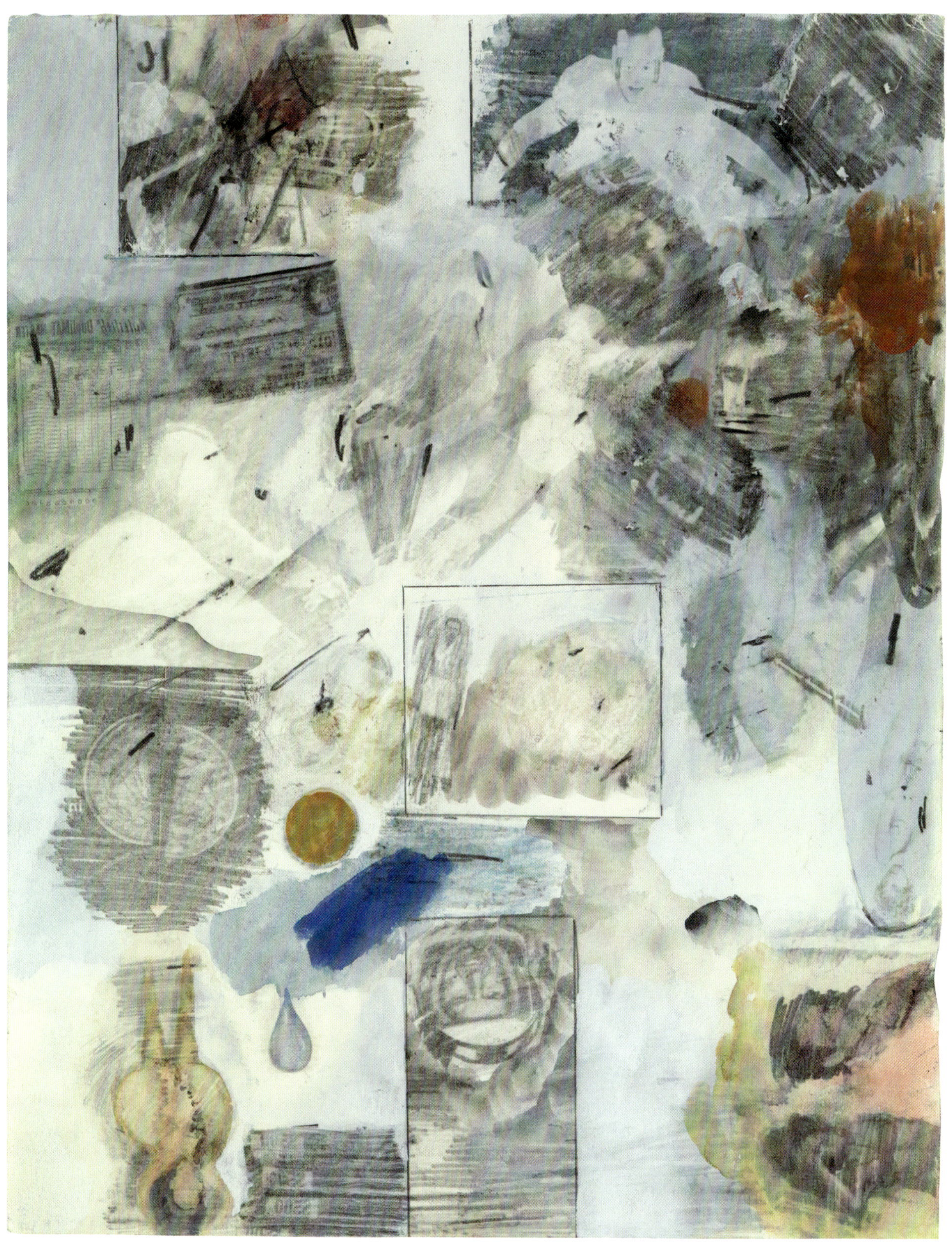

CANTO XXX: CIRCLE EIGHT, BOLGIA 10, THE FALSIFIERS:
THE EVIL IMPERSONATORS, COUNTERFEITERS, AND FALSE WITNESSES. 1959–60
Solvent transfer drawing, watercolor, gouache, and pencil on paper, 14 1/2 x 11 1/2 in. (36.8 x 29.2 cm)
The Museum of Modern Art, New York. Given anonymously

Canto XXXI.

Same first wound.

Blood rushing to my cheeks.

The soothing remedy: touch.

Our backs on the valley.

Crossing in silence.

Less than night, less than day,

Making out a little

(through the gloom).

The path, the sound.

The blood rout.

I stare through obscurity. It's natural

that you should miss the mark.

Clearly, your eyes mislead you.

Take my hand, let me explain

the shapes.

R.C.L.

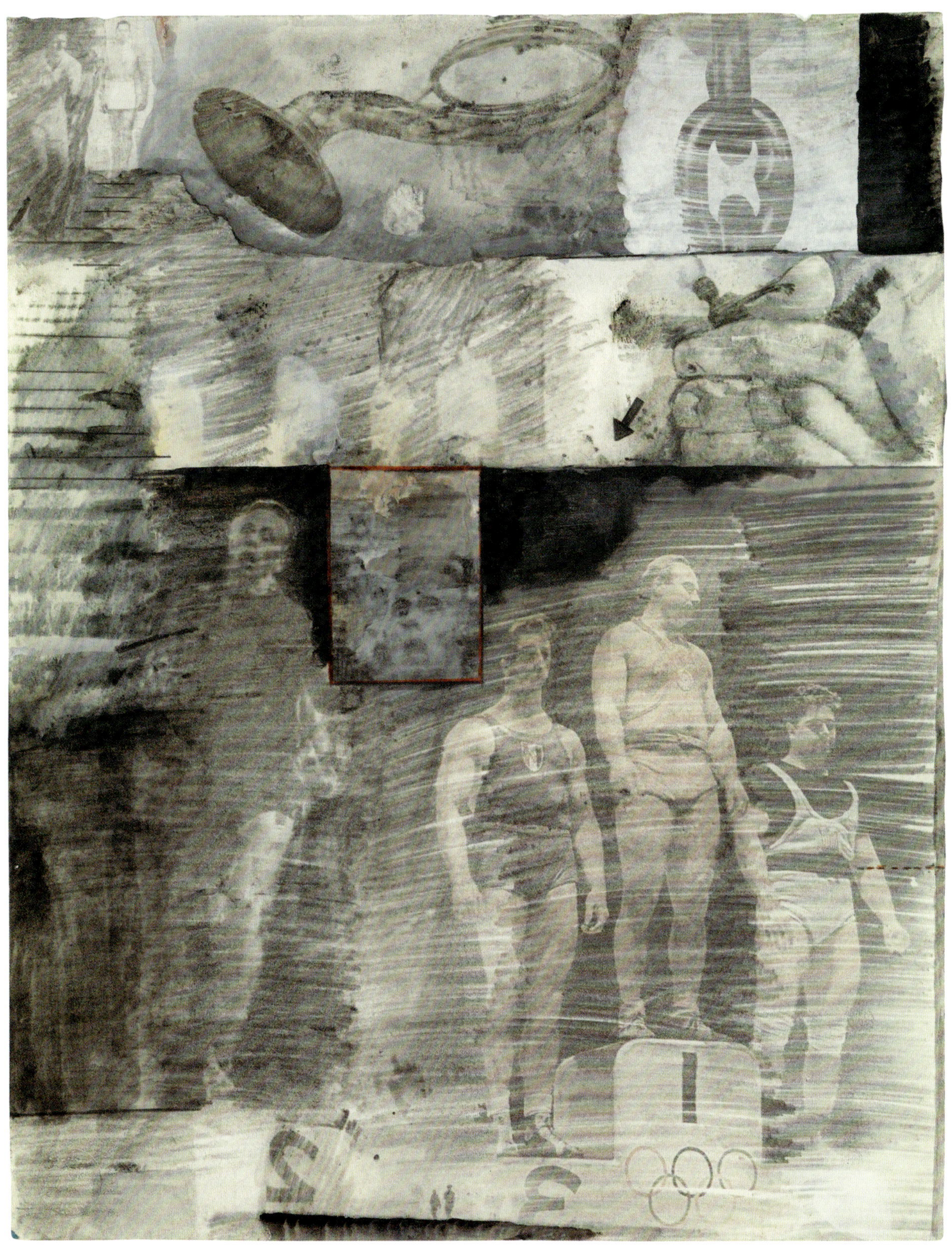

CANTO XXXI: THE CENTRAL PIT OF MALEBOLGE, THE GIANTS. 1959–60
Solvent transfer drawing, colored pencil, gouache,
and pencil on paper, $14^{1}/_{2}$ x $11^{1}/_{2}$ in. (36.8 x 29.2 cm)
The Museum of Modern Art, New York. Given anonymously

Canto XXXII. from *Ninth Circle*

The season stolen—
        the cold comes
without a word.

I wish you would—

I save all the smallest
        things, which, one day
I'll braid into a bloom

        that tries to live
beyond these bare rooms.

✶

How the soul
        slanders the body—
calls it

        a vessel
or temple, either
        way empty, unful-

filled—
        How the body
buries the soul—

        rends & does
not mend it, broken
        like a spirit

        or the soul's shiny
bones, which grow.

✶

The dead grow more
        distant each day
like their fingernails,

or the future.
        Nights, nearer—
squint & you

can see them. The dead
        visit in the taint
between sleep

& waking, between being
        a body & being
aware of one, the shades

        shutting out
no more light.

K.Y.

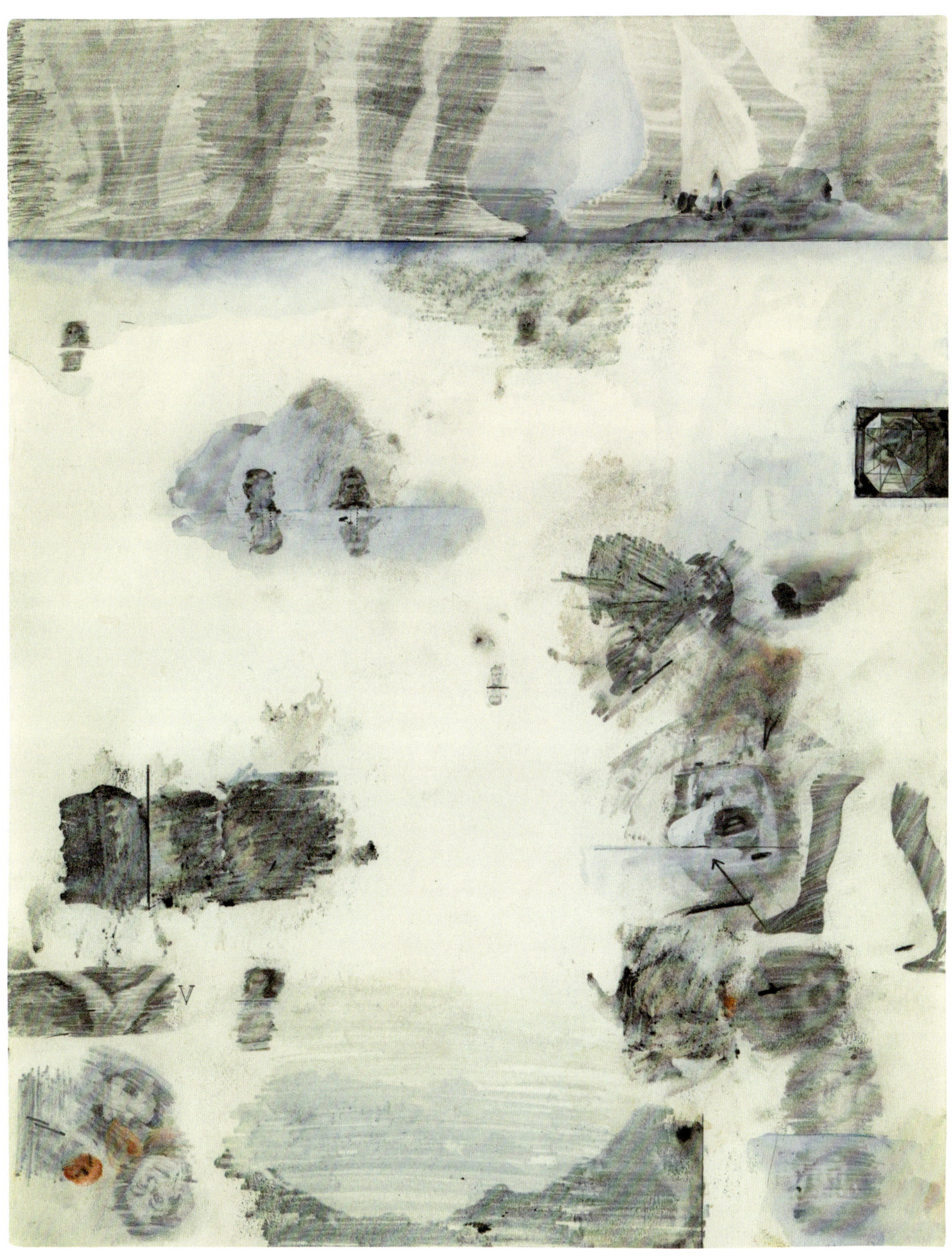

CANTO XXXII: CIRCLE NINE, COCYTUS, COMPOUND FRAUD: ROUND 1, CAINA, TREACHEROUS TO KIN; ROUND 2, ANTENORA, TREACHEROUS TO COUNTRY. 1959–60
Solvent transfer drawing, gouache, watercolor, and pencil on paper, 14 1/2 x 11 1/2 in. (36.8 x 29.2 cm)
The Museum of Modern Art, New York. Given anonymously

Canto XXXIII. *Cocytus*

Do the dead know.

Where they are.

Who.

They're through.

With us, above.

Or below.

Our feet sunk.

In shadow.

The body.

We barely know.

Or own.

They speak like the leaves.

Rustling.

Holding onto the tree.

Wintering starlings.

A bee trapped in honey.

Their very tongues.

Undone.

K.Y.

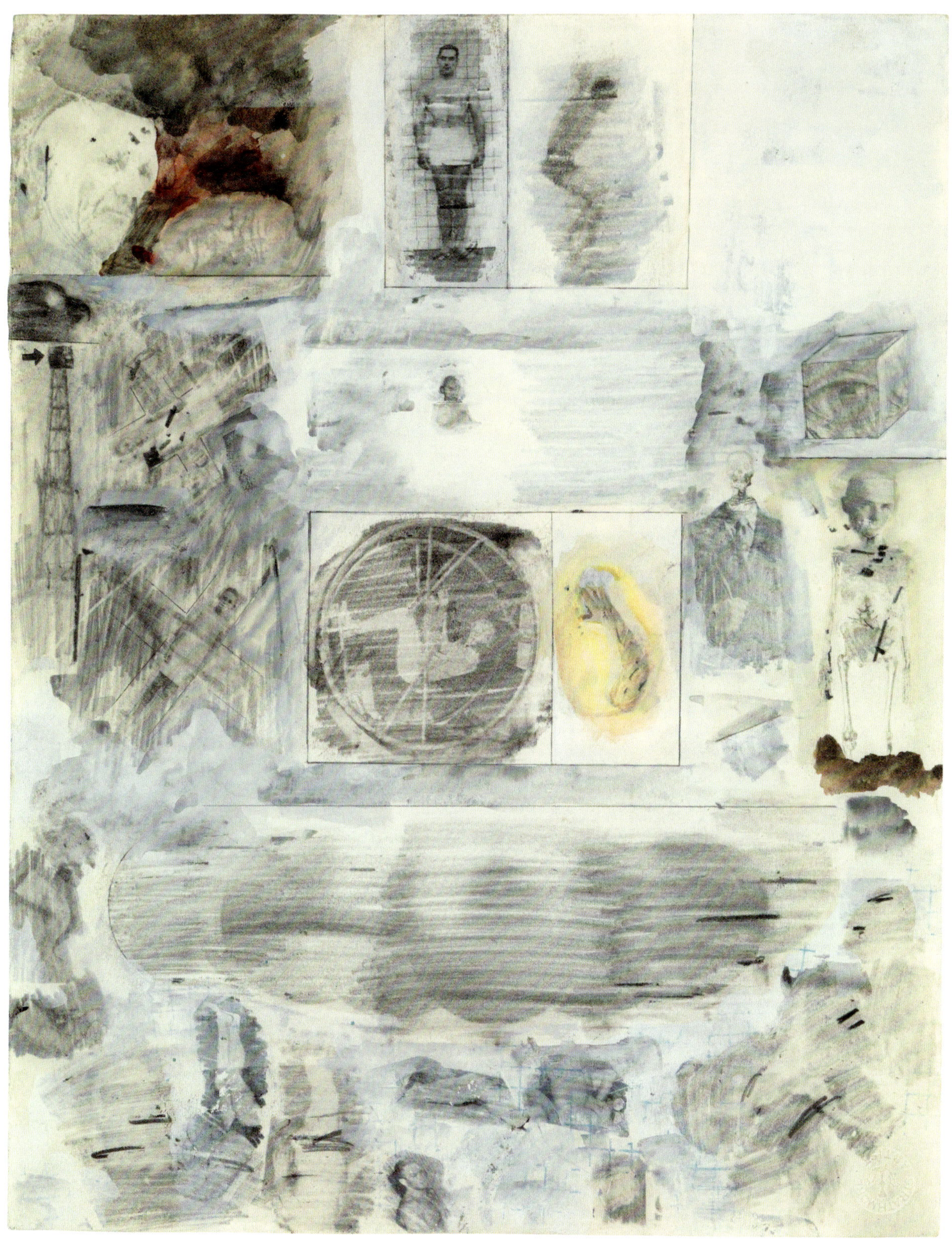

CANTO XXXIII: CIRCLE NINE, COCYTUS, COMPOUND FRAUD: ROUND 2, ANTENORA, TREACHEROUS TO COUNTRY; ROUND 3, PTOLOMEA, TREACHEROUS TO GUESTS AND HOSTS. 1959–60
Solvent transfer drawing, watercolor, and pencil on paper, 14 1/2 x 11 1/2 in. (36.8 x 29.2 cm)
The Museum of Modern Art, New York. Given anonymously

Canto XXXIV. from *The Hotel of Hell*

Each eve he eats
        his friends face first.
I wondered

was that worse? to see just
        where we're going
or to be devoured

by the feet, bottoms
        up, watching
how far we'd come.

The crossroads where
        I take my leave
from him—

an eggshell walking west.
        A knife with legs,
ears pierced with arrows

& the sea a shallows.
        Short-fingered, fickle
as a cock, a cuckold, a fraud—

a goat with a tire
        round its neck.
On the wall a dirty bed.

*

A cold fire. I climbed down
        his slouched
& suited, unsuitable back,

the tower he made
        of himself, his Hotel
of Hell. The night

manager. The manger.
        He turned
away all—

no matter whether the lady
        were full with child,
radiant, hailing

from the middle
        of the world—
the Lord.

Him scared
        of staircases
& saints.

*

Down I scaled, reader,
        escalatoring
till I passed

the point—the equator—
        the loin—
where the Devil's

legs & everything else
        was now
upside down.

I found myself alive in a city
        without angels,
that Easter Monday, alone

in a land that might be ours—
        street covered in scat, all tar—
the graffitied gravestones—

& looked up, peering
        past the haze
through which I thought

        I almost caught
the stars.

K.Y.

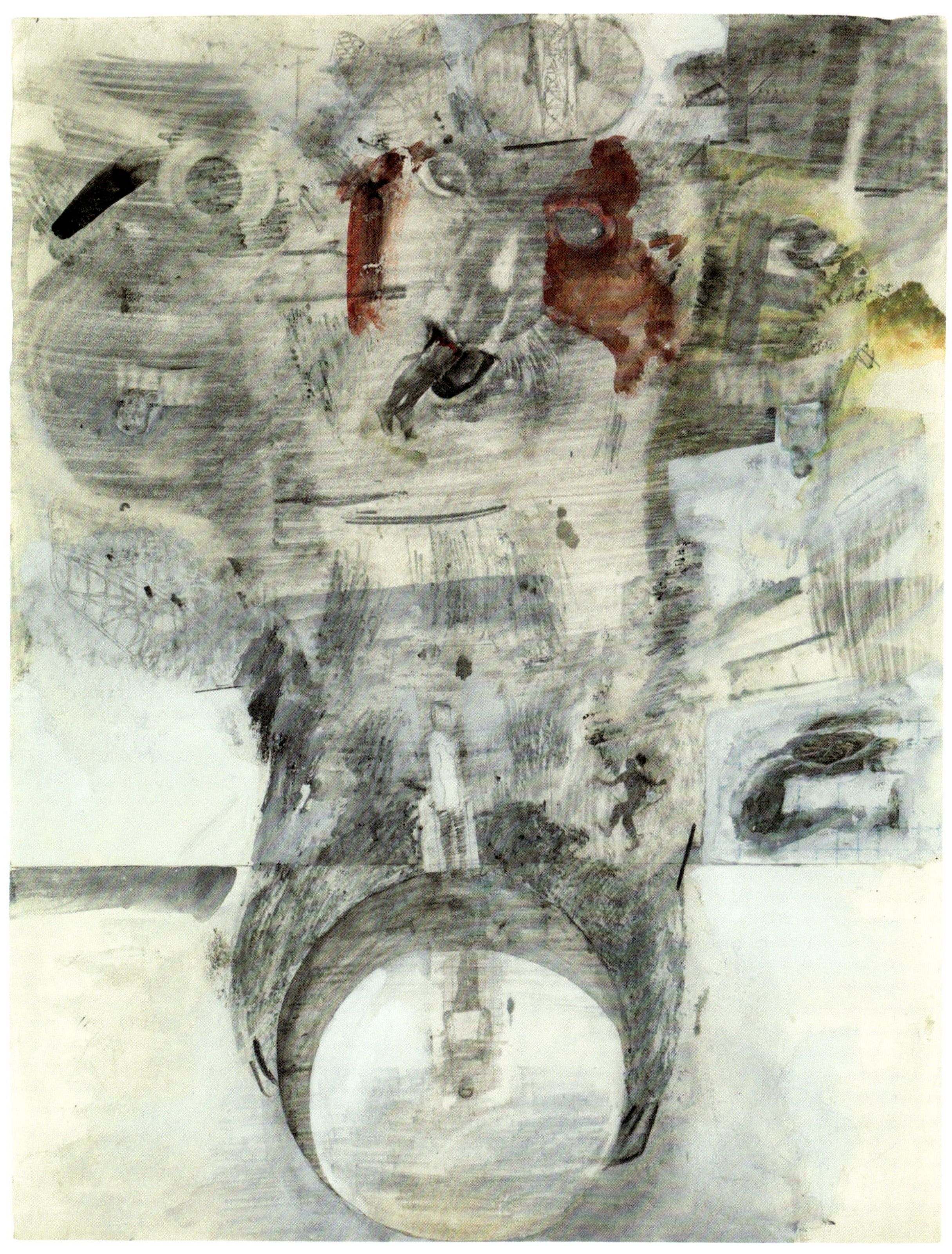

CANTO XXXIV: CIRCLE NINE, COCYTUS, COMPOUND FRAUD:
ROUND 4, JUDECCA, TREACHEROUS TO THEIR MASTERS. 1959–60
Solvent transfer drawing, gouache, watercolor, and pencil on paper, 14 1/2 x 11 3/8 in. (36.8 x 28.9 cm)
The Museum of Modern Art, New York. Given anonymously

Canto Summaries for Dante's *Inferno*

Michael Sonnabend

A self-taught scholar of the Italian Renaissance, Michael Sonnabend was a welcome resource for Robert Rauschenberg as he worked on his drawings for Dante's *Inferno*. Born in Buffalo, New York, Sonnabend had gone to Italy as a young man to learn Italian in order to read Dante in the original. After Rauschenberg completed the drawings, he asked Sonnabend to write a summary for each canto of Dante's epic. Sonnabend would recall that he worked in conversation with Rauschenberg, writing a text a day for thirty-four days straight. Rauschenberg hung the resulting texts below the corresponding drawings when they were first exhibited at Leo Castelli Gallery in New York in 1960. Sonnabend's summaries are reproduced here courtesy of the Sonnabend family; the typewritten originals are housed in the Archives of American Art at the Smithsonian Institution as part of the Leo Castelli Gallery records collection.

CANTO I

Midway through the maze of his life Dante is lost in a forest of tears. He wanders through the darkness of night. At dawn he reaches a hill at the edge of the forest. He looks up and sees the light at the top of the hill, bright with the rising sun. Suddenly his way is blocked by three beasts: a leopard, a lion, a she-wolf. He despairs. As he turns back and rushes headlong downward to the sunless woods, an apparition appears. It is Virgil. He has been sent by the powers of grace to lead Dante to the light. But the way must lead through Hell, then through the sacramental ways of Purgatory, until at last, purified, Dante with the guidance of Beatrice, will rise to the City of God.

CANTO II

The day fades and night gathers all creatures into sleep. It is the night of Good Friday. And Dante alone must face his awesome journey. Like Christ on that night, he must sweat the sweat of his night of agony. At the thought of the pain that awaits him, he loses confidence. To restore his wilted courage, Virgil explains how he came to be on the scene while Dante was rushing downward to eternal loss. He tells how a lady of Heaven descended into Hell, the presence of angels in her speech. She asked him to lead her friend Dante to safety. It was Beatrice. She tells how she heard of Dante's plight in the Court of Heaven. The Blessed Virgin, Mother of Compassion, was first to know. She called Lucy to her presence. Lucy, Patroness of Divine Illumination, was sent to the next link in the chain of grace, Beatrice, to tell how her devoted Dante was fighting against eternal death on the shores of the inner river, over which the sea has no power. On hearing the news of Dante's mortal danger, Beatrice rushed down to Limbo to beg Virgil's help. Having heard Virgil's account of this miracle of grace, and his reproaches, Dante's fears melt. In the warmth and light of heavenly grace, his heart fills with gratitude and courage. A new strength surges through all his being.

CANTO III

The gateway of Hell with its inscription of doom frames a mirror image of Hell. A swirling storm of pain and loss gathers in Dante's ears. When his eyes separate individual souls, he sees the uncommit[t]ed. They march in an endless parade behind the whirling banner of the uncertain: tepid souls who cannot enter Hell nor leave it. As if all were caught in a revolving door that leads nowhere; squashing their souls with the anguish of forever being uncommit[t]ed, forever without place, without form. Beyond the vestibule of Hell, Dante comes to the shores of the Acheron where the damned gather. Charon in his boat tries to stop Dante from embarking. He is foiled by Virgil's magic words. Unlike the uncommit[t]ed, the damned, for all their terror and cursing of life, have the eagerness of the guilty to experience the meaning of their guilt: the limits of their own fullest commitment. Fear of Hell turns into desire for Hell. Charon ferries his cargo of sinners to their eternal fate. The earth quakes, flashes vermilion upon a ghastly sky. Dante, soaked in the sweat of all agonies, falls into a bottomless swoon.

CANTO IV

Dante is awakened from his swoon by a clap of thunder. He has been lying on the brink of the abyss that gathers the echoes of all grief. Virgil, pale with pity, leads Dante down to the first circle of Hell. Here the souls of a great multitude of pagans live on without pain but with a hopeless yearning for divine light. As Dante and Virgil advance, a voice from the distant light rings out, welcoming Virgil home. Then the poets see the approach of a group of master poets of antiquity: Homer, Horace, Ovid, Lucan. These ancients elect Dante, the modern poet, to be sixth among his peers. They approach a noble castle circled by a gentle stream. They walk upon this sweet water as upon firm ground, and continue through seven gates until they reach a flowering meadow. Solemnly gathered in this elysian field are the great spirits of the past, bathed in the radiance of the heaven of the mind. Virgil points out the masters of a vanished world, while Dante drinks in the glory of it. From the stillness of this noble humanity Virgil leads Dante into the roar of Hell.

CANTO V

Dante and Virgil reach the circle of carnal sinners where Minos sits in judgment. Minos wears a ghastly grin as he whirls his tail; a grin that relishes his precise knowledge of the specific gravity of sin within each soul. At each judgment, the grin seems to set in motion a vast, coiling tail circling about his body and stopping with the crack of a magic whip that pinpoints the place where the soul must forever work out the pattern of its choices. Dante and Virgil by-pass Minos and come to the ledge of carnal sinners, bare of light. Within a roaring of hellish winds, vast flocks of the lustful are whirled and battered about in never-ending flight. Virgil points out famous lovers of the past: Cleopatra, Semiramus [*sic*], Helen, Tristan and a myriad of others who chose voluptuousness as their paradise. All are spinning in a storm of passion which they chose as the law of their inmost being. Paolo and Francesca float out to Dante on fragile wings of passion, as a pair of doves. They breathe their tale in tears. Love and death seized them unaware at the same instant. God gave them what they wanted: they are still in love, forever at the mercy of the winds of doom. Dante is overwhelmed with pity. He falls as the dead fall dead.

CANTO VI

Dante comes to his senses in the midst of new torments. A foul mixture of snow, hail, and black rain pelts down through the gloom upon sinners damned for gluttony. They lie immersed in a vast field of freezing, fetid slush. Gluttons who once feasted luxuriously now wallow in the mud. They chose the belly. Now each is all belly. Their symbol and the presiding genie of [the] place is the swinish three-headed dog of Hell, Cerberus: red eyed, greasy beard and a vast swollen belly. His claws rip the howling sinners apart while they squirm about in their slush. Virgil throws Cerberus a fistful of the mush. And while the monster is busy devouring his food, the two walk on, their feet sinking through the sodden mess of bodies and mire. Suddenly a spirit sits up in his slush and asks to be recognized. It is Ciacco, a politician known to Florentines as 'The Pig'. Ciacco is beyond recognition, so he tells his townsman who he is, the nature of his sin, and goes on to tell of the oncoming civil war between Ghibellines and Guelfs. Just as Ciacco is sunk in the passion of his own appetites, so Florence will stew in its own corruption. Greed, envy, and pride will rip the wretched fabric of the city apart, as Cerberus mangles the gluttons. The political theme joins with the theme of individual destiny to be fused at the end of the canto by the angel's trumpet of judgment. As Ciacco rose from his mire, so the dead must rise on the day of judgment to hear the echo of their doom rumbling through eternity.

CANTO VII

"PAPE SATAN PAPE SATAN ALEPPE". The space between the circle of gluttons and the avaricious is filled with this gibberish of Plutus. The bloated guardian, once Lord of Wealth, is countered by Virgil's words of magic power that pierce the swollen brute like an enormous bladder of wind. Plutus collapses and dissolves. The way is open to new agonies. Dante sees a weird choreography of souls dancing out their chosen damnation. They are the avaricious and the wastrels. A great throng of sinners move toward each other from opposite directions in a half circle, yelling, and shoving great weights with straining chests. As each completes his half circle he crashes against an opposing sinner. One group shrieks "Why fling away?" The other shrieks "Why hold so tight?" Then they turn back until another half circle is completed to crash again. Fortuna, the angelic intelligence, stands firm with her wheel in rainbow space. The imperturbable goddess links this group with the next group of sinners: the wrathful and the sullen.

Just as with the wastrels, and the hoarders, the wrathful joust against themselves, squandering their feelings; while the sullen souls, hoarding their feelings under muddy waters, bubble to the surface their hymn of melancholia. They wasted their lives in the sweet air gladdened by the sun; now they must live in the sadness they chose. Fortuna, God's providence, standing between all the episodes, serenely turns her sphere as she tastes her bliss.

CANTO VIII

Dante and Virgil reach a tower on the shore of the Styx. They see mysterious fires flash from the top of the tower, and an answering flash from a distant shore. Suddenly Flegias, the boatman, races across the water to them. Virgil forces angry Flegias to ferry them to the metropolis of Hell. As the boat ploughs through the river of the dead, a wrathful spirit rises from the filth. It is Filippo Argenti, a Florentine, man of blood and bestial arrogance. He questions Dante, clutches at the boat, and they exchange words of anger. For the first time, with savage scorn, Dante increases the torment of a soul in Hell. And Virgil for the first time, with word and deed, pushes a pleading soul back into his filth. At last Dante has grown to a new maturity: in the poet of divine love stirs divine wrath. And it is divine wrath that sets the sinners in the Styx upon Filippo Argenti, ripping him to pieces. Filippo turns upon himself and tears at his flesh with his own teeth. Even the devils at the gates of Satan's city are angry. All Hell explodes with wrath: human, satanic, divine. Throngs of demons angrily refuse passage through the land of the dead to Dante and Virgil. They slam the gates in Virgil's face.

CANTO IX

All the angers explode in the Styx. Now anxiety and fear fills Dante and Virgil. Man, reason, nor the magic power of words can cope with the satanic mind that rules there. As expectation hangs on hope, a sudden vision of horror draws Dante's eyes to the top of the molten-red tower. Three hellish furies have risen: three women bathed in blood, their hair writhing with broods of snakes. They glare down at Dante, shrieking, their nails clawing at their bleeding breasts. All yell for Medusa, the Gorgon, to come and turn the terrorized pilgrim to stone. Virgil quickly forces Dante to turn and shields his eyes with his own hands. Facing the heart of horror, this is the most that man can do. Now only Heaven's messenger can open the way. He appears: first in a clap of thunder that rocks all Hell, then as a whirlwind imperiously roiling its tower of dust, shattering whole forests before it and scattering the wrathful in the Styx like terrorized frogs. Dry footed, he crosses the waters, and with majestic instancy puts an end to the insolence of Hell. One wave of his wand and the gates of Dis are opened. Their way is free. Enveloped in the holy wrath of the angel, Dante and Virgil enter the undefended city of Satan.

CANTO X

Dante and Virgil walk among the tombs of the heretics, where lie those who staked everything on the certitude that soul dies with body. Here in their bed of fire they must forever know the error of their choice. Intellectual pride takes the shape of an iron temple, burning molten red from a fire that never yields to the light. Dante is still in awe of Farinata Degli Uberti, Ghibelline chief. A towering figure, he rises from his tomb drawing all Hell upward with him in his haughty contempt. In his talk with Dante, the defeat of his political goals, of his party, and of his banished family burns more fiercely than his bed of fire. Cavalcante, father of Dante's best friend, rises on his knees in the tomb when he hears the poet, and looks around to see if his son is with him. Love for his son, Guido, and pride in his genius, is the very core of his being. When he thinks that Guido's eyes no longer bathe in the sweet light of the sun he sinks back into his tomb. Now Farinata and Cavalcante cannot escape the knowledge that in their intellectual pride they have denied eternal life to what they have loved more than themselves. After the last judgment the future is forever closed to their proud intellect.

CANTO XI

Once inside the city of Satan, walls, towers, gates, temples, disappear. It is not a city—it is Hell: one vast field of hidden wounds. Broken boulders left from the earthquake at Christ's crucifixion circle the rim of the precipice. Dante and Virgil must pause here to get used to the foul stench that rises from the well of sin. They wait behind the tomb of Pope Anastasias [*sic*], heretic. Here they study the map of pain: a brooding meditation that gathers into one blueprint all the tumors of a blighted humanity. Dante is the eager student opening to new knowledge, asking questions to grasp with greater clarity the chart of man's sins carved in Hell. He is all gratefulness for the knowledge given by Virgil of this divine jurisprudence. It will permit him to be judge, like Minos, of his own maze of sin.

CANTO XII

Along the brink of the precipice of lower Hell, Dante and Virgil face the sprawling minotaur who guards the circle of the violent. Virgil plays on his fury until the minotaur, child of a lecherous queen and a bull, plunges and leaps about in a blind rage. They slip by and clamber down the steep cliff of shifting stone, a tumble of rock that fell when Hell quaked while Christ descended into Limbo. This ruin leads down to the Phlegethon, river of boiling blood, that circles the plain below. Tyrants, highwaymen, murderers, stand steeped in boiling blood: they who wallowed in blood must forever simmer in the trail of blood they left in their path. Along the banks of the river gallop long files of centaurs who guard the sinners. Nessus, the centaur who guides Dante and Virgil, names Alexander the Great, who is up to his eyelashes in blood, and Attila, the scourge of God. He names many others as the river grows shallower. They come to a ford, where Nessus carries Dante across on his back. Minotaur, earthquake, centaur and tyrants unite in a single theme: human brutishness that results in mad bestiality.

CANTO XIII

Dante and Virgil enter the wood of the suicides. All is blighted, tangled, dark. Harpies sit croaking among withered trees. The wood fills with mournful wailing that rises from hidden souls everywhere. Virgil tells Dante to break a twig from a huge bush, and he will understand. Dante does so, and the tree cries out with pain. Words and blood hiss and sputter together from the wound, as from a burning log, begging for mercy. It is Pier Delle Vigne, poet and Imperial Chancellor of Frederick II. He was unjustly imprisoned and blinded for high treason. Loss of honor and of his Emperor's trust drove him to suicide. Pier gives a picture of court intrigue and affirms that he never broke faith to his Emperor. He begs Dante to restore his honor among men when he returns to earth. Like all who destroy their bodies he is denied human form. As he tore the spirit from the flesh harpies now tear at his blighted leaves, and from each wound the blood wails its pain. Even after the last judgment, the body will hang from the tree as on its scaffold. Two torn and naked spirits rush past Dante and Virgil, and the wood leaps with black hounds plunging after them. The slower of the two hides in a bush. The hounds spring upon him, tear his flesh apart and carry off his body limb by limb. They are two famous wastrels, frenzied wreckers of their substance, a form of suicide that is forever re-enacted as they are torn and wrecked. The mangled bush, where the wastrel took cover, pleads with Virgil to bring back his torn foliage. He is a Florentine, identifying himself with his city, broadening and uniting the theme of suicide. Just as he had made a gibbet of the lintel over his own door, so Florence tears herself apart with internal strife.

CANTO XIV

Dante and Virgil reach a plain of burning sand. Great herds of naked sinners are everywhere, some lying stretched out, some squatting, and a greater number roaming endlessly under a rain of fire. Flames, slowly, implacably drift down from Heaven over the windless, burning plain. A never ending ballet of agonized hands fight the flames. The giant Campaneo lies blaspheming and defying God, while God's silent presence floats down in flames upon him. It is rebellion for the sake of rebellion. His punishment consists of the seething fire from within, which calls the eternal fire from above. Dante and Virgil come to a red stream, which has its source, Virgil says, far off on the Island of Crete. There stands an old man under Mount Ida. His head is of pure gold: the rest of him is of silver, bronze and iron. Only the right foot, on which he stands, is of baked clay. All but the gold head is split, and out of this split drips an endless stream of human tears that wears a hole through the stone of the mountain, and forms the four rivers of Hell. The ancient under Mount Ida, distilling all human grief, links with the grandiose figure denying God, and with the Sodomites, and the usurers who have chosen barrenness.

CANTO XV

Dante and Virgil walk on the embankment along the stream. Its vapors form a cloud that quenches the flames above. A sinner from a roving band of Sodomites peers upward and recognizes Dante. Slowly Dante makes out the burnt features of his dear old master. It is Brunetto Latini, fifty years older than Dante, poet, scholar, and revered counselor in matters of art, learning and the world. Dante tells him of his pilgrimage to God. Brunetto warns his former pupil of the plotting of the Florentines, which is gathering against him. He fills his pupil with the courage to follow his star until the glorious arrival in the City of God. Dante, whose first impulse was to fling himself down to do him reverence, envelops his old master with gratitude and love. He taught Dante the art of growing into eternity. A whirl of smoke rises across the sand. Brunetto must rejoin his troop before another band of Sodomites sees him. His only request of Dante is to be remembered in his work, in which he still lives on. Then he runs off across the burning sand swift as a champion, who wins the green cloth at the games of Verona.

CANTO XVI

Dante and Virgil, walking on the dike along the river of tears, are within hearing distance of its waters plunging over the cliff to the circle below. Three spirits of a roving band of Sodomites recognize Dante's Florentine dress. Since they cannot stand still under the rain of fire, they turn in an agonized round, twisting their necks upward at Dante, while their feet keep moving in the opposing direction. They are Guido Guerra, Tegghiaio Aldobrandeschi and Iacopo Rusticucci, three statesmen of high authority. They ask for news of Florence. Dante assures them of the honored place they hold in the hearts of the Florentines: and overcome with pity and reverence for these heroes of his youth whom he sees so humbled, he breaks out in a passionate indictment of present day Florence. Grieved by what they hear, they ask to be remembered to the living and give their blessing to Dante. Dante and Virgil continue to the edge of the cliff where the river cataracts into the abyss. Virgil mysteriously asks for a cord that Dante wears for a belt, and throws it out over the cliff. Dante waits in awed expectation to see what Virgil's magic signal will bring. An incredible monster appears, swimming upwards through the dark void.

CANTO XVII

The monster swims up through the abyss of fraud with the slow underwater motion of a deep sea diver. He lands in silence, and settles on the edge of the cliff close to Virgil. It is Gerion: the image of fraud, who swims in spaceless space, through walls, mountains and weapons; who fouls all life. Dante is most terrified by his kindly, human face, joined to a dragon-like body, brilliantly colored, with hairy paws and venomous scorpion tail that swings free in the void. He is the airship that will carry the passengers below. His image holds the weird secret of sins yet to be explored. Gerion is also linked to the sinners who did violence to nature and industry (art). His benign face, the brilliant colors of fraud on his body, relate to the usurers with their money bags hanging around their necks. These bags are brightly emblazoned with the coats of arms of famous banking families. As Dante walks among them, Scrovegni, a Paduan banker, bellows at him, thrusts out his tongue and licks his face as an ox licks its nose. Dante returns to Virgil who is already on Gerion's back. He mounts, and Virgil holds him as a father holds his trembling child, while Gerion swims down through the void. When the roar of the whirlpool announces the end of the flight, Dante sees the moats below. Gerion glides in a spiral past the fires and the wailing, and lands gracefully on the floor of Hell. He sets his passengers down, and takes off again.

CANTO XVIII

Dante and Virgil have landed in the City of Fraud. The stone floor is an enormous cone-shaped plate that funnels toward a central well as to a cesspool. Ten concentric ditches are sunken in this floor, connected by bridges, like spokes of a wheel ending at the cesspool as their hub. The divine comedy begins here the progressive disintegration of all social threads, until their debris, as it were, drain as excrement into Satan's mouth. Pimps, seducers of innocence, and flatterers, occupy the moat. Dante and Virgil look down from the first bridge to naked sinners at the bottom of the ditch moving along like well-regulated traffic, each file of sinners keeping to the right. In one direction the pimps parade, followed by horned devils whipping them on. Moving in the opposing direction are the seducers skipping to the crack of the devils' whips. Jason, majestic Knight of the Golden Fleece, seducer of innocence, walks with the meanest of pimps. Seen from the next bridge, the ditch of flatterers gathers something of this canto and of all that follows. Thais, prostitute, and the oily-tongued promoter, Alessio Interminei, are immersed in the filth of their own flattery. They prostituted life with words. And so Jason, corruptor of innocence through fair speech, and Caccianemica [*sic*] selling with enticing words his sister's youth must sink at last in the excrement that fills the ditch of Thais.

CANTO XIX

As Dante comes to the Bolgia of the Simoniacs his heart flames with anger. He hurls damnation against the greed that prostitutes the sacraments and the holy office. All the ditch is alive with flaming feet, like candles in a church; legs writ[h]ing and kicking wildly in grotesque agony. The bodies of the sinners are stuffed into tubular holes that line both banks and the ground of the infernal tomb. Dante is carried below by Virgil to question a sinner whose legs weep with greater agony. It is Pope Nicholas III. The Pope mistakes Dante for Pope Boniface VIII, who is scheduled to succede [*sic*] him in his infernal hole. And in an inverted crescendo of apostolic succession, he names Clement VII as successor in Hell to Boniface VIII, while he and Boniface must take their place inside the livid stone, further down. Nicholas III confessed that his traffic in church offices fattened his family purse; now he lies head down in an infernal purse, where he chose to bank his soul. He mocked the baptismal font with its waters of grace, kicking his heels at Heaven; now he is baptized in this degraded reversal, while Hell's fire sucks at his feet. The imagery blends with the opening and closing themes of wrath, suffusing the entire canto with an apocalyptic eroticism: the Church, Bride of Christ, is raped and prostituted. She has become the whore of Babylon, locked in fornication with the kings of the earth. Virgil, pleased at Dante's apocalyptic wrath, embraces him and tenderly bears him off to the next Bolgia, like a babe in arms.

CANTO XX

From the bridge overlooking the soothsayers and magicians, Dante looks down upon a solemn procession of sinners weeping silently, shuffling round and round. To his horror he sees their figures distorted: their faces twisted backwards so that their tears stream down their backs. They who once meddled with God's mysteries fore-seeing events, must advance forever with heads twisted backwards. Dante weeps for their distorted humanity. Virgil reproaches him for his pity of these traders in spells and incantations. Then, to divert Dante's mind, he names the most renowned magic-makers of times gone by. As he points out Amphaiaraus [*sic*], Tiresias, Aruns and the virgin seer, Manto, his words open upon scenes of magic. At each name he unfolds a lost world of mythic tales. Indeed all these soothsayers come from the ancient authors, and Virgil's long story of the founding of Mantua corrects his own story in the Aeneid. Dante seems to forget the sinners in his fascination of their magic; while Virgil enjoys describing his native landscape and correcting the medieval image of himself as magician. He names a long line of medieval witches and wizards, astrologers, makers of magic potions and philtres. Before they leave these magicians and astrologers, Virgil unites all the themes with a vast description of the wheeling universe: the clock that tells the hour. A magic that Dante lived by.

CANTO XXI

Dante, writing in exile, remains officially accused of corruption during his term of office in Florence. Now, standing on the bridge over the chasm that holds the grafters, he may have been brooding over the absurd accusation that none in Italy took seriously, not even his enemies. He looks down into a seething mass of black boiling pitch. Suddenly a huge black devil appears in a wild gallop skimming along the bridge on wide-spread wings. On his shoulders is seated a corrupt senator, fresh from Lucca. The fiend tosses the grafter over the bridge into the ditch below where demons suddenly appear to take charge of the new arrival. They tear at him with claws and pitchforks, prodding him like floating meat beneath the seething stew: singing with sarcastic gaiety how the punishment fits the crime. The grafter worked under cover; now he is forever busy at secret pilfering under cover of the boiling pitch. Public funds stuck to his greedy hands; now the pitch sticks fast to his eternal being. Dante remains in hiding while Virgil negotiates with the pack of devils for their passage. Malacoda (evil tail) turns meek at the news that Virgil and Dante are here under divine protection. He informs Virgil that the bridge that leads to the next circle is broken down, and offers some of his devils as escort to another crossing. A squad of ten devils is formed in good military order. Before they start, each sticks his pointed tongue out at their sergeant. Barbariccia (curly beard) taking their salute, makes a trumpet of his ass, and they're off!

CANTO XXII

Never in all his military career, never in his reading of vast strategic movements, has Dante seen or heard of infantry, cavalry or naval expedition start off with bugle blown so low! But never mind: in church with saints, with stewpots in saloons. Dante walks along the banks laughing at the exuberant coarseness of his escort, and with indulgence of contempt for the sinners. He sees a few of the grafters surfacing from the pitch with arching backs like dolphins, or with muzzles showing from the surface like frogs. But all plunge swiftly to cover when the squad appears. All but one, who ducks too late. In an instant he is speared and hauled ashore. The sinner cheerfully tells of his life in Navarra. He was born to rascals, so he came by his genius quite naturally. As he reveals the names of other corrupt officials in the pitch, his roguish talent suggests a trick that will out-trick even the devils. He proposes to lure half a dozen of his cronies out of the stew, if only Virgil can persuade the devils to stand away from the edge of the pool. One of the devils offers to play a cat and mouse game with the Navarrese. If the grafter will dive in the pitch, the devil proposes to catch him on the fly, like a gull swooping on a fish. The grafter leaps free like a shot, plunges into the pitch, while the devil (Alichin) swoops out in full flight, only to miss the clever rascal. Calcabrina (hoar-frost), in a rage at his colleague's foolishness, flies out above the stream and fights with Alichin. They rip and claw each other until they plunge, locked together, into the black brew. The boiling heat breaks up the brawl, and the rest of the squad in great confusion must fish them out. Dante and Virgil take advantage of the confusion to slip away.

CANTO XXIII

There is not time to stop on the bridge over the hypocrites. Dante is haunted with the terrors of the ditch he has just left. It suddenly comes to him that these are not stage devils in a slapstick morality play, but ministers of God's justice. Even Virgil was fooled. The bridges over the entire circle are down. And just as Dante feared, the great wings of the devils swoop into sight. Virgil seizes Dante in his arms, leaps the bridge, and slithers downward into the ravine. At the bottom of the moat, they find themselves in the midst of a slow procession of the hypocrites, weighted down by painted cloaks and hoods, such as monks wear. Outwardly their mantles are gilded, but they are lined with lead. Dante and Virgil walk alongside the sinners, who creep with leaden pace and groan an eternal litany of weariness. Two sinners hear Tuscan spoken as they pass, and call out. They are the jovial friars of Bologna, a Guelf and a Ghibelline, once chosen to head the bi-partisan administration of Florence. Now their crushing burden creaks with what in life was the pompous weight of keeping up empty appearances: a religious pretence, and a dazzling show. Across their path lies a naked figure nailed to a three-staked cross, upon which the sinners tread. It is the supreme hypocrite, Caiaphas. For expediency, he chose rejection of the Cross. Now he is on the rack of the cross he chose, forever bearing the weight of his choice.

CANTO XXIV

The canto opens in a mood of discouragement. Dante is tired. Virgil is disturbed and uncertain. At this point, Dante, in homage to his guide, draws a Virgilian portrait of the peasant who wakes to find the fields all white, and returns to his cot in despair that he cannot take his lambs to pasture. Then he peeps outdoors again, and sees that the sun has melted the hoar-frost and has turned the earth to green. Just so, the mind of Virgil cleared of its doubts, and Dante feels a surging of new strength and hope. Virgil gathers him up in his arms and climbs from the Bolgia of the hypocrites to the top of the broken bridge overlooking the Bolgia of the thieves. A voice fills the darkness of the ditch with rage. They climb down and see a loathsome mass of serpents, gliding, creeping, spiraling everywhere. Among them naked sinners, hands tied by coils of snakes, run looking for a hole in which to hide. As one thief races past, a snake leaps up in a flash and bites him in the neck. The thief flares up into flames and crumbles to ashes, then, phoenix-like, his ashes shape into his form again, and he rises, shaky and bewildered, not knowing who he is and where. Once he made the substance of men vanish; now he must be destroyed and made to vanish over and over again. Questioned by Virgil, Vanni Fucci is overcome with shame to be forced to confess that it was he, a leader of the Black Guelfs, who pilfered the treasury of the Church. By pretending to be a man of blood and rage, he had tried to hide his meaner nature to the world, to himself, and to God. In a rage he takes revenge by giving details of the civil wars that will bring victory to his party, and crush all Dante's hopes of ever returning to Florence.

CANTO XXV

As shame and pride gather and swell in Vanni Fucci, he raises both fists, with thumbs protruding between fingers, and hurls the supreme obscenity into God's face. At this a snake coils itself around the blasphemous throat. Another binds his arm[s] behind him and knots its coils tightly in front of him. He had refused all his life to know himself as God knows him. Now, in death, he has full knowledge of himself. He is Hell's great loser. Speechless, powerless, he flees. Cactus, the centaur, races after him. On his haunches rides a gruesome swarm of snakes; behind his neck a dragon breathing fire, crouches with wings outstretched. Three Florentine thieves appear close to where Dante and Virgil stand. One asks the other why a fourth has stayed behind. In answer to the question a great six-legged lizard hurls itself against one of them. The lizard fastens his limbs to the thief's body with such terrifying precision that the monstrous compenetration mingles man and snake. The snake takes possession of the man, and in turn is possessed; enclosed by what he encloses. From this fusion is born an unnameable monster. Another metamorphosis. A black monster leaps up at another thief, bites into his navel and then falls to the ground in front of his victim. The snake bite is the radiating center from which it will steal the human form, and to which it will transmit its reptile form. Victim and reptile stare at each other. Smoke pours from the bite of the human's navel; smoke pours from the mouth of the sprawling reptile. The two smokes meet and mingle in a single cloud. Eyes and smoke are interlocked in the magic transmutation. An inscrutable operation of God turns man into snake, snake into man.

CANTO XXVI

Dante and Virgil climb the great tumble of rocks from the valley of serpents until they reach the rim that overlooks the next Bolgia, that of the evil counselors. In the chasm are flaming spires wandering along, each stealing away a sinner in its bag of fire. These are evil counselors sheathed in the torment that each spun on earth from the coils of his own cunning. Once they worked in hidden wiles; now they are hidden in the flames of their own conscience. Dante notes one whose cresting flame splits into two horns. These are Ulysses and Diomede, suffering under one flame for their guiles of the Trojan horse, Achilles, and the Palladium. Dante asks to talk to the epic hero, but Virgil alone knows the words that can make Ulysses speak. Virgil asks how and where he died; not about his sins. To Dante, as to Virgil, such sins belong to the stately history of antiquity. Ulysses begins to speak and at once the open sea air carries the tale of the mad voyage that drew him and his men into uncharted waters. After leaving Circe, he and his companions sailed past islands of the Mediterranean, Sardinia, Spain, and Morocco until they reached the Straits of Gibraltar: the end of the known world. Poised at the gates of the unknown, he persuades his crew, now stiff and slow with age, to use their last breath to know all that is knowable and beyond. And though the epic hero's little ship went down because he dared too much, he had stretched his knowledge beyond the limits of the known to the very shores of the mount of Purgatory. Ulysses' quest was Dante's too. But illumined by grace, Dante landed on the shore of the mount of Purgatory and rose to God.

CANTO XXVII

The flaming tongue of Ulysses leaves. Another evil counselor, clothed in flame floats forward. Hidden within moves the shrewdest man of his age: Guido Da Montefeltro, Lord of Romagna. Dante and Virgil hear the muffled voice of a spirit shut so deep within his flame, that the tongue struggling to release its sound vibrates shrilly, like the muffled bellowing of victims burned alive in the brass bull of Sicily. Guido asks for news from his homeland. Dante tells him that war does not flare openly in Romagna; but over his land hovers an armed peace as between wild beasts. The eagle of the Polentini sits restless, brooding on Ravenna's walls; Forli's green lion watches this armistice with suspicion; while the old mastiff, Malatesta, and his pup wait in Rimini to be unleashed. In return for Dante's courtesy, the subtle condottiere presents himself as warrior and Franciscan monk. He tells how he had hoped to end his days in holiness. But he became the victim of his own fame. Pope Boniface VIII, who was waging war, sent for him. In return for a cunning stratagem, he promised absolution in advance for his sinful advice. Through Guido's plan of betrayal, the Pope achieved his worldly ambitions. Guido's spirit wavers forever between a Machiavellian relish in the art of deceit and a Franciscan desire to enjoy God. The warrior died a monk. At his death, Saint Francis comes to bear his soul to Heaven. But the Saint must yield to the Devil and to the judgment of Minos.

CANTO XXVIII

Dante and Virgil look sown [*sic*] from the bridge over the sowers of discord. Here divine justice manifests itself as a gruesome procession of spirits hacked and ripped apart. Mahomet is the first to approach the bridge. He is split wide open from crotch to chin. Between his legs hang all his bleeding guts. Mahomet, sower of religious discord, tells Dante that now [*sic*] only he but all in this ditch are mangled and split apart. As they tore the fabric of society apart, now they are hacked and torn apart. They drag their way round the ditch until they return before a demon with a great sword, who again slashes them open for another round of pain. One sinner with mangled face looks up. Words begin to move along the bleeding gullet of his open throat. He is Pier Da Medicina, sower of political discord in regional wars. He takes a fierce pleasure in ripping open the tongueless mouth of another sinner, Curio, who had advised Caesar to cross the Rubicon and start Rome's civil war. Mosca raises his bloody arms, with hands hacked away, splattering his face with blood. His advice started the factional wars between Guelfs and Ghibellines. Now the blood is on his head. Last comes the strangest sight in all the moat; a body without a head moves forward. In his hand he holds his weeping head, swinging it by the hair like a lantern. He stops below the bridge and stretches his arm upward for the head to speak to Dante. It is Bertrand De Born, great lord and master troubadour. He set Prince Henry of England against his father, Henry II. Now the sower of family discord must walk forever with head severed from body.

CANTO XXIX

The circle of falsifiers is the last of ten concentric rounds of Malebolge. The first round imaged the prostitute Thais sunk in excrement. Continuing as through ten drain pipes circling downward into a cesspool, all the bonds of love and nature become diseased, dissolved, and finally drained into this last ditch of fraudulent pestilence. In this canto, the alchemists, transmuters of metals, falsify things. A sickening stench rises to the bridge where Dante and Virgil stand, and with the putrefaction, such shrieks of anguish, that Dante stops his ears with his hands. They descend into a murky trench of pestilence. Through the feverish vapors, they see the alchemists dumped in a heap: some lying on others, some crawling and writhing on hands and knees and belly; all too weak to raise themselves from the stony bottom. Two alchemists sitting propped against each other like pots, and scrubbing away at their scabs with bloody nails, are startled to see the living Dante walk among them. One is Griffolino of Arezzo. He tells Dante how he swindled a fatuous gentleman of Siena who insisted on being taught to fly. The gentleman had him arrested, and Griffolino was burned for his real crime, alchemy. The other reminds Dante that he is Capocchio, a friend of his school days. Capocchio was known as a reckless, quick-witted prankster and a genius at imitating men and animals. Alchemy also came naturally to him. Along with Dante, all make fun of the madcap Sienese spendthrift rakes, who squander their lives just for the hell of it.

CANTO XXX

Two naked spirits come racing wildly through the ditch. One sinks his teeth furiously into Capocchio's neck and drags him off. It is Gianni Schicchi. He impersonated a dead man, kept hidden, in order to make a will in his own favor. The other is Myrra, incestuous daughter of the king of Cyprus, who disguised herself to couple with her own father. In life, they borrowed the appearances of others for foul ends. Now their fury forever seizes upon Hell's apparitions. Dante gazes at a spirit shaped like a mandoline, with tiny face and neck above a bloated paunch. It is Master Adam, counterfeiter of florins. In Hell, the Florentine has a counterfeit body coined like a water-logged florin. From puffed lips, curling apart and parched with thirst, he pleads with Dante for one droplet of water. His thirst increases forever, as his mind forever lingers on the image of the cooling waters rippling down moist hillsides into the Arno. The counterfeiter names two sinners sitting next to him. These are false witnesses: Sinon the Greek, false deserter, who persuaded the Trojans to bring the wooden horse into their city, and Potiphar, who lyingly accused Joseph. Sinon, offended by this presentation, turns and wallops Master Adam on his swollen belly, and such an animated squabble breaks out between them, that Dante lingers to enjoy the comedy. Virgil is indignant at Dante's self-indulgence, at which Dante blushes with shame. They leave the imposters, swindlers, counterfeiters, liars, and all the brawling imbroglioni of the Italian street scenes, forever stewing in their fricassee of history and of sacred and profane mythology.

CANTO XXXI

Dante and Virgil are on the stone floor of the ten moats, walking toward the central pit, the dead point of life where Lucifer is forever fixed. The gloom and the deep silence is torn by an enormous trumpet blast echoing in Dante's mind back to Roland's horn at Roncesvalles. He stares, frightened, through the dim air to what looms in the distance as a city of great towers. These are the giants and titans who rise from inside the wall of ice, where they stand as Satan's bodyguard. Dante and Virgil come to the towering circle of the sons of earth and sea, their bodies rising sheer from the rim of the well. Nimrod, mighty hunter before the Lord, and builder of the tower of Babel, his hunting horn hanging from his neck, stands like a gigantic imbecile. He bellows some gibberish he himself does not understand. Virgil tells him to use his horn if he has anything to say, since it is he who tangled all human speech. Ephialtes, taller and more savage is bound by an enormous chain around his body, imprisoning his right arm behind his back and his left across his chest. His boldness once put fear into the gods of Olympus when they watched him pile mountain upon mountain to reach Jupiter. But, Antaeus is unchained, and can speak. Virgil appeals to the childish vanity of the giant to lower them down to the ice below. He flatters him like a great lord speaking with respect to the village idiot. Proudly the giant puts out his palm, vast as a delicate steam shovel, lowers these clever little people and tenderly places them on the ice below. Then he slowly rises into place again, like the mast of a ship.

CANTO XXXII

From the sloping bottom of the ice, Dante looks upward at the silent, towering guardians of the well of silence. Then his eyes turn to the vast, mirror clear, frozen lake that holds the treacherous to kin in its grip. It is the circle of Cain. Only the sinners' heads emerge from the ice, bowed forward to allow their tears to fall, while their chilled teeth beat in chorus like a chattering of storks. Among them Dante sees two livid heads so clamped together that their hair is mingled. He asks their names. As the two raise their heads to reply their tears turn to ice and freeze between the eyelids. Maddened by the pain of grief that finds no release in tears, they butt their heads against each other in savage fury. Another traitor names them. They are the brothers Degli Alberti, who killed each other in a fight over their inheritance. He goes on to betray his name and the names of others around him. Treachery, the cold-blooded sin, must live on forever clamped in isolation. Dante and Virgil continue to the circle of traitors to their country: Antenora. As he threads his way among the heads, Dante accidentally kicks a face. The sinner shrieks his abuse at the intruder. Dante grabs the howling spirit by the hair to shake his name out of him. He learns it is Bocca Degli Abbati from a neighbor in the ice. Bocca betrayed Florence at Montaperti. Now frozen in hate, Bocca betrays the sinner who revealed his name. Dante sees two heads frozen together in one hole. The one on top has sunk his teeth into the base of the other's skull. He gnaws at him with the fury of a starving man crunching a crust of bread. Dante asks him the reason for such devouring hate, promising in exchange, to proclaim the justice of his cause among the living.

CANTO XXXIII

Count Ugolino raises his mouth from his ghastly feast, wiping the blood on the hair of Archbishop Ruggiero's skull. It is grief and love, gnawing with a hunger that can never satisfy its hate, that forever binds the two traitors. Ugolino serves as God's instrument of justice by which a killer by starvation serves as food for his victim. In life Ruggiero and Ugolino ruled jointly in Pisa; and both betrayed Pisa. Ruggiero then betrayed Ugolino. He had the Count and his four sons imprisoned and left to die of starvation. Count Ugolino's story slowly unfolds in a cell of Pisa's tower of hunger. Dreams of foreboding; the nailing of prison doors as of a coffin; the father's suffering as he looks on helplessly for days and nights as each child dies of starvation before his eyes; all end with Ugolino's blind groping from body to body through two more days and nights, calling, calling, each child's name until hunger stopped a breathing that had become all grief. Dante walks on to the circle of traitors to guests: Ptolomea. Here the sinners lie flat on their backs. Their tears freeze in the eye sockets, turning grief inwardly to anguish without exit. Friar Alberigo is induced to reveal his shame, and a punishment special to this circle alone. He invited cousins to be guests at a banquet of reconciliation, and murdered them. From that very moment, while still alive, the body of Alberigo is occupied by a demon while his soul plumbs straight to hell before the body's death. Dante had promised Alberigo to clear the ice from the cavity of his eyes and release his tears. But his story told, Dante refuses, adding that to be rude to this soul was courtesy.

CANTO XXXIV

Dante and Virgil peer through the foglike mist, and see what appears to be a vast windmill looming in the distance, stirring up an icy wind. All about them is silence, rigidity, and mirror-black ice of the circle of Judas. Traitors to their masters are covered by the frozen lake strewn in contorted postures and shining through like straws in glass. Once they swore special allegiance to their masters; now they are completely sealed off from every motion, every contact. The Emperor of Hell slowly emerges in his terrifying bulk as Dante and Virgil arrive where the ice grips him at the navel. Dante, neither dead nor alive, gazes at the towering head with three faces: red, yellow, and black. From each pair of eyes flow tears that mix with blood and froth. Under each face moves a pair of bat-like wings, giant sails rising and flapping to generate a freezing wind. In each mouth he chews a sinner: Judas, with his head inside the central mouth; Brutus and Cassius dangle from the yellow and black faces. The Emperor of Hell wanted to be God. Now he has his wish. He is a ghastly reversal of the Triune Godhead: the Father, the Son, and the Holy Ghost are now impotence, ignorance and hate. Once he was the fairest of the sons of light, a seraph with radiant wings, breathing in the warmth of God's love; now he is a self-crucified mountain of flesh with bat-like wings, generating cold winds of hate that forever grip him tighter in his prison of ice. Virgil, with Dante clasped to his neck, descends along Satan's matted flanks, until they reach the socket of his haunch where they seem to be climbing upside-down and back to Hell. They have crossed the center of the earth: the absolute pole of evil, where gravity is reversed. They toil upward guided by the sound of the hidden river of Lethe trickling down to the frozen lake. Dante and Virgil emerge at last to see the stars again.

Trustees of The Museum of Modern Art